Scarsdale
Apr 10 1963

For my friend and admired
photographer
John D Schiff

Sincerely
James N Rosenberg

CLOUDBURST: Oil, 1954: Metropolitan Museum of Art, New York

Painter's Self-Portrait

JAMES N. ROSENBERG

EDITED WITH AN INTRODUCTION BY MILTON S. FOX

PUBLISHED BY CROWN PUBLISHERS, INC.

NEW YORK   1 9 5 8

FIRST PRINTING
LIBRARY OF CONGRESS CATALOG CARD NUMBER: 58–11411
ALL RIGHTS RESERVED BY THE AUTHOR
PRINTED AND BOUND IN THE NETHERLANDS

DESIGNED BY MARSHALL LEE

INTRODUCTION

This is a book which many people have literally badgered into existence. For a long time it seemed to many of us who are engaged in the arts that the many-sidedness of James N. Rosenberg should be brought into a single field of vision, but with the focus on his art, for that has become the central, indeed the overriding, activity of his later years.

This *Painter's Self-Portrait* is the consequence. For its author it has been an arduous labor, since there have been in his life several careers, any one of them rich enough for a book. There is the story of one of the country's most notable bankruptcy and reorganization lawyers; there is the story of an imaginative public servant who applied daring and furious zeal to national and international missions for humanity; there is the story of a model sportsman and conservationist; and there is the long, long story of his battle for art in America, which has not slackened up to this very moment, in his eighty-fourth year. He has sacrificed a lot of telling, so that the central theme of art stands clear. What might have been *My Life Story* is more accurately and fittingly titled *Painter's Self-Portrait*. The cost, in energy and time, has been considerable, what with the cutting, pruning, deleting, rewriting; but the greatest cost, the hardest one for us to take, is the cost in lovely canvases not done with the same time and energy.

James Rosenberg has been painting for almost fifty years. For at least ten years now he has been a professional artist in the sense that he has given most of the working day (and many, many working nights) to thinking, studying, supporting, and creating art. This astonishing man, who was a gifted amateur during the remote era of the William Howard Taft presidency, turned professional at the age of seventy. And though his work has changed much since the early pictures reproduced in this book, he has never painted better than in these last few years, with a boldness and vigor, a technique and a vision which are still arresting despite the fact that most of his work is within what Sunday newspaper critics call "accepted idioms.

He has always remained attached to the world around him, a painter "for whom the visible world exists." It is refreshing in this day when so much of painting is disturbing, self-mutilated (cutting away so many of the attractions which, historically, painters have offered us), or just plain sterile (however stylish it may be), to come upon the frank, direct, and accomplished landscapes of a man who is awed by mountains and storms, enchanted by Spring and falling waters, and inspired by the forest vastness.

"The majority of Rosenberg's works are landscapes," wrote John Coolidge, director of the Fogg Art Museum, in his introduction to the artist's one-man show at the Fogg in 1950. "This is a comparatively unpopular subject among American painters today and most contemporary landscapists either use nature as a point of departure for abstract compositions or copy her photographically with or without surrealist overtones. Rosenberg by contrast wishes to represent the forces of nature. His interest is not in the configuration of an individual hill or the shape of a single tree, but in the vibration of light in the autumn woods, the slanting drive of rain, or the eerie effects of moonlight. There is little variety of place but much of mood. . . . Rosenberg uses many techniques to differentiate these moods: pastel to convey the oppressive moment just before the break of a storm, irregular dabs of pure color to represent autumn leaves, pulverized mica mixed into the pigment to suggest the glitter of snow. . . . It is his search both for vividness and for intimacy which determines the personal quality of Rosenberg's art. That quality has brought him recognition by American museums, some twenty of which include his paintings in their permanent collections."

Today the artist's works are not only in museums, but also in many private collections, embassies, colleges, libraries, hospitals. Nobody—and least of all Rosenberg himself—knows how many or where they all are. He has been an extraordinarily prolific painter, and a generous one. Through purchase or gift most of the country's great museums—the Metropolitan, the Museum of Fine Arts in Boston, the Cleveland Museum of Art, the Fogg, the Smithsonian Institution (which holds art for the National Gallery of Art in Washington until it becomes eligible for inclusion), and others, have acquired his work; and the list of regional collections where he is represented is impressive. A few names at random: the Joslyn Memorial Art Museum of Omaha, the Nelson Gallery-Atkins Museum of Kansas City, the Walker Art Center of Minneapolis, the Georgia Museum of Art in Athens, Georgia, Smith, Bowdoin, Tel-Aviv, Brandeis, and Harvard colleges, among others.

I have said earlier that Rosenberg has always remained attached to the world around him, whether in the north woods or in Israel. But he does not let us forget that this world includes also some crimes against humanity so vast and gruesome that only an age of refined technology could be guilty of them. And to those circumstances he has responded with characteristic vehemence—for he is entirely unlike those painters who seem to create their landscapes or abstractions solely for the purpose of withdrawing into them. Instead, he has boldly faced the facts of life, as he has faced the facts of nature. Depression, mechanization, tyranny and brutality—the outrages and violences of human origin—all have stirred him deeply, just as the violences and dark moods of nature do. And in some of his pictures, notably those done after the trip to the Ardennes, there is a savage contrast of moods in a grim marriage of youthful death and springtime youth.

Rosenberg is not gentle or subtle or "pretty" in his paintings of the "Ironism," "Atomism," or "Korean" series, all represented in this book. They are frank, unabashed protests, anguished and pained, and what could under other circumstances be called crudeness of technique should be seen here as contributing to the raw urgency of the protest—in the same way that the great Expressionists gave urgency to their vision with their strident color and brushwork. Note this about Rosenberg's art: how remarkably he uses his repertory of technical means according to the subject and mood of the work. W. G. Constable, who recently retired as curator of painting at Boston's Museum of Fine Arts, said in a catalogue for the Rosenberg show at Wildenstein's in 1947 that for this painter "the world is a complex of phenomena resulting from vast underlying movements of which man himself is equally a consequence.

He is always striving to express an underlying unity behind the visible world—not a comfortable, harmonious unity, but that of a dramatic resolution of tempestuous forces. That, I suggest, is why the term romantic fits his work, since the thing seen is always interpreted in terms of a personal conception of the pattern of existence. It is this that provides an essential link connecting the very varied types of work he has produced. The series of lithographs inspired by the slump that rocked the United States; the paintings of Pittsburgh witnessing the triumph of what he calls 'Ironism' in man's affairs; the 'Atomism' paintings here exhibited, foreshadowing what may be man's future in the grip of yet greater powers, are in essence cut from the same kind of cloth as the paintings made in the Adirondacks. . . ."

This is also noted by Charles C. Cunningham, director of the Wadsworth Atheneum, in another of the artist's exhibition catalogues: "Even in a fundamentally tragic painting . . . he cannot resist a tulip or two in the foreground to show his faith in tomorrow's springtime." Rosenberg is indeed "a romanticist and poet," as he was called by the distinguished, just-retired director of the Cleveland Museum of Art, William M. Milliken.

The point is, simply, that Rosenberg is an artist, with the instinctive painter's gift for somehow being able to distill what he sees and feels, and then transmuting it into pigment. But pigment to which he gives magic life and spirit, and uncommon richness, for he is a colorist primarily. Though the majority of the illustrations in this book are in black-and-white, the colorplates will still suggest how varied, sensitive, and radiant his color can be in the joyous moods, and how somberly deep and expressive in the darker.

One regrets that the author has left unrecorded in this book so many of his triumphs, failures, hopes, thoughts, and experiences. They are encyclopedic in range, often hilarious, and always fascinating. But no man has ever given himself more wholeheartedly to art; when he isn't "promoting" American art with his customary zeal and resourcefulness (he calls this his "unfinished business"), he is usually to be found in his studio surrounded by canvases awaiting his touch.

It is therefore finally right that he should appear before us as an artist, painting and fighting for art in our world, and especially in our own country where now so many are ready to ignore that art has freed man from physical confinement long before the first sputnik beeped its way across the sky.

M. S. F.

FOREWORD

When in 1921 Dr. Abraham Rosenbach exhibited my pictures in Philadelphia, he asked me for a statement to be printed in the catalogue. Where and under whom had I studied; what was dragging me from courtroom to canvas; were my diverse activities reflected in my paintings? Such were the questions with which he plied me. "If my pictures have merit," I wrote in reply, "they will stand on their own feet. If not, nothing I write either about myself or them will be of interest."

Since I believe that the visual arts must in the long run communicate to the beholder and gain recognition only on their own worth, I adhere to the views I then expressed. If therefore this were only a picture book, there would have been no foreword, no story, and for that matter, perhaps no book at all.

I have, however, been prevailed on by good friends in the world of art to attempt this self-portrait of a painter, in order to tell if possible what made me forsake that jealous but rewarding mistress, the law; explain how the paths and by-paths I trod and still tread, and the battles I have engaged in during my long years, weave into my pictures.

My life never having been lived in separate, water-tight compartments, it has been difficult to decide what is relevant, what is immaterial. Cézanne, the great master, freed himself from all things except art, which, as he once put it, "might hook him tight." Deeply as his life and works have influenced me, I have never been able to lock the world out of my studio. Hence the story which follows.

J. N. R.

CONTENTS

ILLUSTRATIONS

The Story

1. THE FIRST DECADES

On Buena Vista Street (an appropriate place for birth of a landscape painter) in Allegheny City, Pennsylvania, now part of Pittsburgh, I entered this planet on November 20, 1874. So vast have been the changes in the brief span of eighty years since that horse-and-buggy post-Civil-War era of President U. S. Grant, that my birth might as well have happened centuries earlier.

When I was five years old our home was at 114 Sheffield Street. There I lived with my parents, sister Minnie, grandfather, and my great-aunt Tante Karline, who ruled the roost. At dusk of a winter evening, my nose glued to the window, I watched silent snowflakes falling. "Why," I asked my mother, "are they black when I look up at them and white on the sidewalk?"

That snowstorm, vivid as if of yesterday, suggests

how from childhood nature's ever changing moods have been essential themes of my landscapes which were to come. The flicker of aspen leaves which my pictures have never yet caught; "walking rain," as the Indians described wet winds which veil my beloved Adirondack peaks; sunset behind Hurricane Mountain; gray dawn over Camel's Hump thirty miles away which gets me shivering out of my Adirondack Shanty Brook bed: such are perennial happy sources of most of my paintings—except those of later years, which began with my 1929 lithograph *Dies Irae*.

In 1848 my grandfather, Louis Naumburg, born in 1813, emigrated from Germany to this country in search of a land of freedom. Scholar, poet, teacher, dreamer, musician, he became the Cantor and officiated as Rabbi of the Synagogue Rodeph Sholom in Pittsburgh. He reached the ripe old age of eighty-seven. By the time I was five years old he had filled my mind with Bible stories and taught me the Hebrew alphabet. When the Hebrew Union College of Cincinnati made me an honorary Doctor of Hebrew Letters, I was able to pronounce only the first three letters of that ancient—and now in dynamic Israel, living—alphabet. But that the seeds of my forefathers' faith took deep root, this story will reveal.

My first art effort took place in Tante Karline's kitchen, where I watched house painters stroking white paint on grimy walls. When they adjourned to the back yard for their lunch hour, I had my chance. Tante Karline was marketing. I was alone. On the stove stood a big bucket containing a cooling liquid designed to become a cheesecake. I dipped a painter's wide brush into the golden cheesecake mixture and splashed glorious color over the kitchen wall, the stove, the floor, and myself.

Tante Karline was not an art lover. Freudians might say that the painful event which occurred when she caught me yellow-handed and splotched from head to foot put a lasting block on the infant artist. Long years elapsed before I took to paint brushes again. I have never since used cheesecake as a medium.

In 1879 the Rosenberg family moved to New York. My parents forsook the strict rituals of orthodox Judaism, joined the Ethical Culture Society, headed by Felix Adler, and sent me to Ethical classes. But the Society's "deed, not creed" principle omitted all the deep emotional content which I believe to be the basis of religion, and left me cold. Until my entrance into The Gunnery School in Washington, Connecticut, when I became thirteen years old, I ceased to be aware that I was a Jew. And even then, Sunday mornings, when I had to attend the Congregational Church, were my only contact with religion. Thus I lost something which I believe is rarely captured when not implanted in earliest childhood; hence my religion is perhaps suggested in a couplet which, while an undergraduate, I composed for my secret self: "Let others go to synagogues or churches. I worship God beneath His pines and birches." Those lines seem to me to shed light on my painting life.

ABEL AND MONET

Ever since the summer of 1887, when a black-bearded Heidelberg University Doctor of Philosophy named Ernst Abel took two Goldmark boyhood friends and me to Keene Valley in the Adirondacks, those tree-garmented mountains have been and are my favorite place in the world. Snow-topped Jungfrau, Mont Blanc, gaunt treeless Mount Atzmond (loftiest peak in

Israel), Mount St. Peter from which, in 1926, I descended to Yalta on the Black Sea, the melodramatic crimson, orange, and purple cliffs of Corsica which Jo Davidson and I in 1934 tried to catch with rapid water colors, have no such magic for me as have the green-blue-purple Adirondacks, the autumn gold of their birch trees, and the scarlet of sugar maples mingled with dark pine and spruce trees.

Abel, who later tutored me for Columbia College, which I entered in 1891, not only instilled in me the love of mountains and mountain climbing, but also taught me to collect beetles and to house them in a container made out of discarded cigar boxes. On rainy days he directed my long labors of putting it together with tiny nails and glue.

Beetles often hardly bigger than a thumbtack-head guard themselves so well by protective coloration that keen searching eyes are needed to find them. Thus at Keene Valley I acquired use of two indispensable tools, eyes and hands. Eyes can train themselves not only to see but to remember. Though I have never visited Cascade Falls in Keene Valley since 1888, I need only close my eyes to behold those tumbling white waters as if I stood beneath them. Hundreds of such pictures are in my mind.

At thirteen I was underweight and undersize. Despite his humble means my father sent me to The Gunnery, a boarding school which I recall with fondness. There I took art lessons from Miss Shuttleworth, with whom I fell in love. I have an 1888 charcoal drawing of tulips which my proud mother had framed. It is my only art record until 1910. When I left The Gunnery in 1889, Miss Shuttleworth made me promise to visit the Metropolitan Museum of Art.

The Connecticut hills, valleys, houses, brooks, and rivers, all of which became deeply a part of me, remind me of Grandma Moses, who has with clarity and directness pictured

TULIPS : Charcoal, 1888 : The artist

the tranquil world of my boyhood—a world my grandchildren will never know.

At The Gunnery began my first lifelong friendship. Alfred L. Kroeber, having come from a then noted Jewish New York private school (whose headmaster was the uncle of Paul J. Sachs), our schoolmates deduced that Kroeber must be a Jew, ostracized him, and branded the Nordic youth with hateful epithets. Why I escaped mistreatment I do not know. While it served only to entertain Kroeber, it brought back to me awareness that I was a Jew. It is something I have hardly ever since then forgotten.

On my return to our New York home I remembered Miss Shuttleworth and became a frequent visitor to the Metropolitan Museum, becoming a member in 1919. Meissonier's *Friedland*, of which Manet once remarked that "everything is steel in the picture except the cuirasses," Rosa Bonheur's *Horse Fair*, and the Inness and Wyant landscapes were among my earliest favorite paintings.

In about 1893 the American Art Association (now Parke-Bernet), housed then at Twenty-third Street, held an exhibition of French Impressionists. Kroeber and I (twenty years ago I painted a portrait of him) journeyed from Forty-ninth Street and Madison Avenue, the then small home of Columbia College, our Alma Mater, to Twenty-third Street. Startled by Monet's amazing colors I damned him at first as a fraud who sought to capture the public eye. But his colors kept haunting me. I returned to Twenty-third Street. Solitary walks in Central Park and along Riverside Drive followed in search of Monet's mauves, purples, lilacs, blues, golden greens.

Somehow I discovered that if you spread your legs wide apart, bend far forward and with your head upside down squint at the landscape through outspread legs, you find shapes, designs, and colors you have never before seen.

Why does this ridiculous posture help vision? Do the laws of gravity bring energy into optic muscles? Or is this upside-down view so divorced from habitual seeing that trees, hills, mountains, valleys, skies, become wondrous form and color never before seen? I still squint upside down at the landscape. Words cannot express what I owe to Abel and Monet.

COLLEGE

Entering Columbia in the autumn of 1891, I had the luck to come under the spell of a great teacher. In the ensuing four years I took every course given by George E. Woodberry. Inspired by him I devoured prose and poetry, studied the aesthetic writings of Spenser, Coleridge, Shelley, Pater; especially Aristotle's *Poetics*. I have never forgotten Aristotle's axiom that "art is the expression of the general through the particular" or his discussion of the *katharsis* through pity and terror.

Woodberry turned me to writing; I became a founder of and frequent contributor of prose and verse to a college magazine, *The Morningside*, for which I also drew posters to attract subscriptions. One of my sonnets found its way into Edmund Clarence Stedman's *Anthology of American Poetry*. I composed the script for a stillborn operetta; made friends with lively and gifted contemporaries; learned also that the doors of fraternity houses were locked against me; refused to join a Jewish fraternity because I did not—and do not—believe that such separatism is good for us humans. I then weighed only one hundred and two pounds but soon learned that I had no chance against an Alpha Delta Phi classmate to become coxswain of the freshman crew.

The Smart Set and *Everybody's Magazine* published my stories. These and book reviews for the *Globe, Bookman,* and the New York *Times* literary section not only began to help the Rosenberg family budget but turned my thoughts to a life of letters. The climax of those literary efforts was a superb five-act drama in blank verse about the French Revolution which I tried to read to Woodberry at his 5 East Seventeenth Street home as we sat before a blazing hearth. When I fell fast asleep over my *magnum opus* before I got halfway through the first act, I became aware not only that I would never rival Shakespeare, but that I was not meant to be a writer (a truth which has weighed heavily on me during my long labors in composing this text).

Having become a Bachelor of Arts, a highly appropriate degree as I did not then perceive, the choice of a career stared me in the face. I had spent summer vacations working (at no pay) for Bierman, Heidelberg & Co., a large clothing firm in which my father was credit man and head bookkeeper. The life of business repelled me.

During my senior undergraduate year I visited the courts to listen to Joseph H. Choate and other leaders of the bar. Their battles had much to do with the first of those crucial decisions which mould men's lives. I entered Columbia Law School, graduated, and was admitted to the bar in 1898. At law school I met a classmate, Wilbur L. Ball, who later became my law partner. It was a lifelong, never-clouded friendship which ended only with his death.

Long before college days an enduring friendship had also begun with Carl L. Alsberg. In college Joseph M. Proskauer made the Kroeber, Alsberg, Rosenberg trio into a quartette. In summers we camped in the Adirondacks and climbed their peaks. In 1897, Proskauer and I published a book of Columbia undergraduate verse dedicated to Woodberry.

Alsberg, who became a noted scientist, died in middle life; Kroeber, in youth an imp of mischief, is one of our country's most noted anthropologists. Proskauer is one of our foremost lawyers. They all stuck to their professional careers. Did inner conflicts bedevil them as they did me?

YOUNG LAWYER

In 1898, through my father's help, Mr. Sol Kohn, lawyer for the clothing firm of which my father was an employee, gave me my first job. The salary was nothing per week and I was set to bookkeeping instead of to law. To my father's dismay, four weeks of this and of the condescending Mr. Kohn were all the impatient young lawyer could stomach. Telling Mr. Kohn that I had not spent four years in college and three more in law school to become his unpaid bookkeeper, I abruptly went my way.

Soon I found another clerkship where at five dollars per week I was set to the revolting task of trying to gouge payment of doctors' bills from impecunious patients. This job too I soon threw up. My third position paid ten dollars per week and gave me a wealth of legal experience. Though my employers were fine men and good lawyers I was determined to strike out for myself. Perhaps they were not sorry. One of the partners had handed me a copy of Elbert Hubbard's then celebrated *Message to Garcia*, instructing me to take it to heart. I did so and had the effrontery to hand him "a messenger's reply," in which I let my five employers know what I thought of them. In that period of history Huyler's Candy Stores advertised their candies as "fresh every hour." So was I.

On January 1, 1900, Proskauer and I formed our own law firm. Our first case was one in which my father was plaintiff and the clothing concern for which he had given most of his life's service was defendant. In the years to follow, I was to be engaged in far greater lawsuits. But never had I a part in a case more compelling than Rosenberg versus Heidelberg. We won it. Mr. Sol Kohn was the defendant's lawyer.

THE COLUMBIA UNIVERSITY CLUB

In 1900 Frederick P. Keppel, a college mate—many years later head of the Carnegie Foundation—invited me to become a charter member of the Columbia University Club in process of formation. When he informed me of objection because I was a Jew, I promptly had him withdraw my name to relieve him from embarrassment. Thereupon he asked me to let him propose me for membership as soon as the Club was formed. I would at once be elected a member, he assured me. After the Club came into being he unhappily confessed that the anti-Jewish issue had again arisen. I declined to have my name withdrawn a second time and was blackballed. It was an event which, as will be seen, had a considerable bearing on my life as a painter.

On May 3, 1956, there came a sequel to this old story which is not entirely irrelevant. Out of the blue I received a letter from the chairman of the Club's Admissions Committee inviting me, "at the suggestion of Dr. Grayson Kirk" (Columbia's President), to join the Club. "Being now eighty-one years of age, most of my Columbia associates are no more," I replied. "I hope it will not be regarded as ungracious of me to decline an invitation which would have gladly been accepted had it come a half century ago."

Am I straying from the theme of this story? Let my life—especially my pictures after the rise of Hitler—answer. Not my Adirondack landscapes. I have never encountered anti-Semitic sunshine, storms, trees, brooks, forests, or mountains.

BESSIE

August 12, 1904, was by all odds the most important day of my life. On that day, at the Twin Mountain House in the White Mountains, I met a girl named Bessie Herman. As we sat together that afternoon in a little ivy-covered summer-house beside the Amanoosac River, I almost proposed marriage then and there. I did not even leave her for five minutes to see whether trout were rising—a statement which those who know my infatuation for brooks and for *salvelinus fontinalis* will find hard to believe.

On November 22, 1905, we were married in Boston at the appropriately named Elysium Club. Rabbi Fleischer who officiated asked me for the wedding ring, which I had bought the preceding day; he examined it closely and noted three tiny letters incised inside it. The letters were "S.C.L." "S.C.L.," asked the Rabbi, "what do these letters mean?" "Sympathy, Congeniality, Love," I promptly replied. I had purchased the ring from the Boston jewelry firm of Shreve, Crump and Low. More than a half century has gone by. My impromptu reply to the Rabbi was prophetic.

In 1904 a prominent lawyer named Abram I. Elkus hired Proskauer and me as clerks, assuring us that if we made good, we would become junior partners. Among the firm's clients were leading United States textile merchants, who, having long been robbed by dishonest bankrupts, had formed the "Merchants' Protective Association" in order to cooperate in helping honest debtors to their feet pursuant to the 1898 Bankruptcy Law; but also to punish frauds. Their immensely varied legal work in these fields was placed in my inexperienced hands and was conducted by me at a separate office at 346 Broadway, near many of the textile establishments.

Scarcely had I started this work when two things happened which powerfully affected my life for the next forty years. A man named Kanter landed in the bankruptcy courts heavily in debt to my clients. A leading admiralty lawyer named Charles M. Hough was appointed Receiver. There was little more for him to receive than Mother Hubbard found in her cupboard. Kanter's daring frauds roused the textile community. I was called on for action. Through months of piecing together evidence I built up a case of grand larceny against Kanter which led to his indictment.

Assistant District Attorney James W. Osborne, who tried the case for the prosecution, had me sit beside him during the trial to brief him on the complicated financial details of Kanter's swindles. The then noted lawyer Max D. Steuer, who defended Kanter, tried to make me the defendant, charging that as lawyer for powerful U.S. textile merchants I was using the District Attorney to force poor, ignorant little Kanter to pay my rich clients. Kanter was convicted and went to jail. It was the first such successful assault on crooked bankrupts in years. Thus I suddenly became a sort of hero in the textile community.

Any industrious lawyer of fair intelligence could doubtless have accomplished what I did. Yet, wholly unaware as I was of what that case had in store for me, from that time until four decades later, when I finally forsook the courts for canvas, I was continually called into bankruptcy cases. During the course of that case Receiver Hough and I grew to be sworn friends. When he became a federal judge his faith in me was a major element in my life as a lawyer. I worshiped him. It was his inspiration which led me to write legal articles published in a law book dealing with corporate reorganization and proposing new laws (later enacted) to achieve full, equal justice among majority and minority interests alike.

The bankrupt who owed a few thousand dollars was a despised creature from whose troubles most reputable lawyers shied away. But the insolvencies of corporations which owed millions were horses of a different color. Such corporate downfalls were not looked on as bankruptcies, but were cases for "reorganization," attracting leaders of the bar.

A minor depression in 1907 and its resulting reorganizations promoted me into membership in the aristocratic reorganization bar. That advance, assisted greatly through cases entrusted to me by a prominent banker uncle of mine, Elkan Naumburg, brother of my grandfather, meant big fees in days when there were no income taxes, and also yielded considerable prestige. Recklessly I bought a home at Coles Lane, Far Rockaway, Long Island. It was a large old house with a larger new mortgage. Without a thought of the morrow I repaired the house and spent every dollar I had earned; also I became father of our first child, Elizabeth. Anne and Robert came later.

Though I continued to visit the Metropolitan Museum, I had formed a special liking for etchings and in 1908 began attending auctions where I ignorantly acquired trash. They turned out to be enormously valuable investments, for it was in New York that I met and renewed acquaintance with an Adirondack Keene Valley boyhood companion, Paul J. Sachs. How epochal an event this was will later appear.

When in 1909 my wife's sister Sara was being married in Boston, my search on the wedding day for etchings resulted in my purchase of thirty-five prints by Rembrandt, Dürer, Ostade, etc. The white-haired, aristocratic dealer who owned them specialized in Washingtonia but had long ago, he said, picked up a lot of etchings by chance from the estate of a very proper Bostonian. He said he knew nothing about them, but thought there were some Rembrandts, and he would sell them at three dollars apiece, all or none, if only he could find them. Would I care to visit him? "Yes, I would," said I. So I climbed with him to the top floor of an old mansion across the street from the golden-domed Boston State House. Up on a stepladder rummaging through his shelves he finally handed me a dust-covered brown paper package.

Breathless, I tried to untie and finally cut the strings, sat down on a dust-covered chair and looked at thirty-five prints. On the back of each was a bit of faded writing which told how the deceased Bostonian had picked it up in Paris in 1807.

Here was the collector's dream come true! My heart nearly burst through my shirt front. On the walls were hundreds of Washington portraits. I had no eyes for them. I offered my check for $105, as I had only ten dollars in my pocket. When the cautious dealer declined my check we proceeded together to the 424 Marlboro Street house of Joseph M. Herman, my father-in-law, an outstanding Boston shoe manufacturer, whose check the dealer was willing to accept. Despite the frenzy of preparations for the imminent wedding Mr. Herman listened for a half-minute to my story and handed the dealer his check for $105. "Remember that I am selling them as is," said the gentleman, and departed.

"As is," my father-in-law echoed, and refused even to look at my treasures. "You don't know these Yankees. You have bought a lot of rubbish," said he. Two days later as soon as I got to New York I visited my expert friend Fitzroy Carrington, who remarked that my delightful Rembrandt duck was flying in the wrong direction. Etchers will at once know that my "Rembrandt" was an etched copy. Carrington's pleasantry about the ducks flying to the other side of the picture gave me no comfort. The thirty-five prints were perhaps worth twenty-five cents apiece as curiosities.

Mr. Herman, from whom it was useless to conceal the truth, declined to let me pay the price of my folly. But a series of telegrams bombarded me from Boston, the first of which offered me "thirty-five magnificent Japanese prints. Great bargain. Hocuspocusai."

That misadventure not only put an end to my print collecting, but resulted in an action the import of which I did not foresee. Art had become an irresistible magnet. Why not create rather than collect? I bought a printing press and paper and all the paraphernalia of an etcher. Rembrandt's drypoints looked so easy to make. At Far Rockaway I spent my evenings making etchings. I destroyed every print I made and got rid of the press. I was not very happy.

And then one day Monet popped into my mind. I began looking upside down at the landscape, bought a drawing pad and a little box of colored chalks and experimented

with them. I got a big thrill. Undeterred by my law partners'
caustic comments, I spent my three-week 1910 summer vacation at a seven-dollar-a-week Woodstock, New York, boarding
house. I was a student in an art class conducted by John Carlson. Every day we pupils went out into the fields and painted
little pictures of hills and church steeples and barns and trees.
Neither Carlson's teachings nor his paintings appealed to me. I
still have my first oil painting. It is a mountain. It is not reproduced in this book. All the others went into our fireplace,
which has been fed by hundreds of my efforts.

When I got back to Far Rockaway, Bessie was eager
to know what I had learned. "I am done forever with art classes
and art teachers," I told her. Nature, I asserted, was to be my
one and only teacher. Have I stuck to this? What of Michel-
angelo, whose definition of the process of art as the "expurga-
tion of superfluities" has had an immense influence on me; of
Aristotle; of Abel and Monet; of Woodberry; of life's countless
impacts upon my palette? Most of all, perhaps, what of Cézanne, that humble, profound student of nature whose works
I began to study?

Though I continued to be a hard-working lawyer
with plenty of exciting law cases, I built myself a studio adjoin-
ing our Far Rockaway home, bought oils, watercolors, pastels,
charcoal, canvases, an easel, and became not only a Saturday
and Sunday but also an evening electric-light painter. Problems of design and form, of color to give form and substance
and dimension, absorbed me. It was a magical escape from the
dog-eat-dog battles of bankruptcy practice; a delightful avoca-
tion. Little did I comprehend that it would reshape my life.

In 1911 a small art shop on West Seventy-second
Street owned by a man named Katz gave me my first one-man
show. A newspaper mentioned a bankruptcy lawyer who
painted pleasant little pastel landscapes. Another hoped I was

better with a brief than with a brush. Never mind. I had made a start.

OUT FOR MYSELF

Whether it was my increasing attempts at art or the fact that Mr. Elkus did not relish being looked on as a bankruptcy lawyer, or that he had warned me more than once to keep a ton of lead in the seat of my trousers, stick to the law, and not be too big for my boots, by 1912 he had had enough of me and of the bankruptcy department. With his generous blessing I took the bankruptcy practice with me, lock, stock, and barrel, and formed my own firm, which was appointed legal adviser to the group of textile houses for which I had worked during eight crowded years. My law practice grew by leaps and bounds. Never again did I become a junior partner, despite several flattering proposals. Never from that day did I feel called on to justify or explain my excursions either to my easel or to other extra-legal adventures which, as the years sped by, played ever increasing roles in my life and finally took me over completely.

In 1912, when I was thirty-eight, there came to me the U.S. Motor Receivership. This was my biggest case up to that time; it was presided over by Judge Hough. When its reorganization in 1913 created the Maxwell Motor Company—now Chrysler—George W. Davison, chairman of the reorganization committee, invited me to abandon the law, move to Detroit (at a large salary and a stock bonus), and become the company's head. This was another of those crucial moments which make or mar a man. What, I wonder, would have happened had I accepted that tempting proposal to become an industrial leader? Success or failure? Leader? Or slave? I declined the offer. Somehow, I had the sense to realize that to accept would have meant farewell to the kind of life I wanted to lead.

Two years later, while I was engaged in the many-million-dollar Claflin bankruptcy, a very different crisis arose. On a Thursday morning the newspapers headlined a story that a junior law partner of mine named Robert P. Levis had been indicted, charged with having conspired with bankrupts to defraud creditors who were my clients.

This being the very kind of crime which it was one of my principal duties to ferret out, I felt it my duty to offer my resignation as attorney for the association of merchants which I had been serving for eleven years. I did so at once at a meeting called by me and attended by some fifty leaders of the textile industry. Though they stood by me to a man, refusing to accept my resignation, my firm was under a cloud. My partner Wilbur L. Ball, calm, steady shock absorber, and Bessie and my studio were my refuge during dark days and sleepless nights.

The court soon threw out the indictment as wholly without foundation. But there followed further assaults on me and my firm by bankruptcy lawyers who wanted those textile merchants as clients. The climax of those unhappy months came when Grenville Clark, a lawyer of highest standing, was retained by a textile client to examine into one of the small bankruptcies which poured almost daily into my office. It quickly became only too clear both to him and to myself that the case had been woefully neglected by my office.

Though Clark generously refused to let the incident be made into an issue, the suffering I had for months undergone had brought me close to a breakdown. The fear that any one of my law associates or clerks might stumble or blunder or neglect a case hung over me like a nightmare. Though well aware of the cost it would be to me, I determined that I had to set myself free. This meant nothing short of resigning my attorneyship for the important association of merchants and forgoing all its benefits as soon as I could in good conscience part from friends and clients who had loyally stood by me.

WORLD WAR I AND SEVERAL DIVERSIONS

Our entry into World War I in 1917 gave me the longed-for opportunity to say good-by to the association of merchants for which I had worked during fourteen eventful years. It was a sad good-by. While some of those merchants continued to be my clients, the daily influx of bankruptcy cases came to a sudden end. Free of the daily grind which had nearly overwhelmed me, I kicked up my heels like a colt in a pasture, painted like mad, and plunged into war work.

President Wilson appointed a banker, Albert H. Wiggin, brilliant builder and head of the Chase Bank, to the chairmanship of the New York branch of the U.S. Fuel Administration. This meant control over use and distribution of much-needed coal throughout the entire state and included the important task of bunkering of ships in New York's harbor. Mr. Wiggin, for whom I had done some legal work, selected me to be his lawyer at a dollar a year.

Scarcely had we entered upon our duties when an emergency confronted us. Seventeen ships lying in New York's harbor which were to carry our munitions and soldiers overseas had to have coal which was in New York but which, we were told, had been promised to Canada by no less a person than President Wilson himself. Dr. Harry A. Garfield (former President of Dartmouth, or was it Williams?) was national head of the Fuel Administration. None of his many regulations and rules explained what we were to do.

Taking the bull by the horns, we held the coal and telegraphed the story to Dr. Garfield, stating that (Canada notwithstanding) we intended, unless overruled by him, to bunker the seventeen ships with that coal. We waited forty-eight hours, wondering whether we had committed *lèse majesté* or would be indicted. No answer came. We bunkered the ships. Whenever thereafter in doubt about our powers we invariably wired Dr. Garfield, telling him what we were about to do. Never once did there come an answer. My only punishment was that (so far as I recollect) I never received my dollar from Uncle Sam.

As Special U.S. Assistant Attorney General (another dollar-a-year task), I won conviction of the German Catering Company for hoarding sugar in violation of the Federal Wartime "Lever Act." The case, brought by instruction of Herbert Hoover, then Federal Food Administrator, resulted in his knowing me, a contact which was to have immense consequences.

Saturdays and Sundays I kept for myself in my Far Rockaway studio. In 1917 the Ferargil Galleries exhibited my paintings for the benefit of the Red Cross. Some were sold. In 1918 Judge Hough procured my appointment to go overseas as a colonel in the Judge Advocate's office. I felt almost cheated when the armistice of November 11, 1918, arrived before I could set sail. Also, I became the lawyer for the Theatre Guild, having sat in Phil Moeller's apartment when he, Lawrence Langner, Rollo Peters, and Lee Simonson gave it birth. It was a stormy delivery. Much later I helped Eugene O'Neill and Kenneth MacGowan form the Greenwich Village Theatre. Those were entertaining escapes from bankruptcy practice. So was an address of mine at the New York City Bar Association (which owns the largest Adirondack landscape I ever painted), wherein I attacked a 1915 U.S. Supreme Court decision approving censorship over the movies and even over the newsreels. I argued that that wartime decision was in violation of the Bill of Rights. Freedom of thought, expression, and art was then and is still an overpowering credo of mine. In peacetime the Court later reversed itself.

The extent to which art was fighting for ascendancy over me during these years is indicated by a little two-act play I wrote entitled *Return to Mutton*, published in 1916 by Mitchell Kennerley. Though I did not realize it, that playlet was a sort of autobiography of the lawyer, the artist, and the lady. John, a middle-aged lawyer who has become a judge (always the dream of most of us lawyers), Jane, his young wife, and Augustin, a young artist, create a typical triangle. "Mutton" was the busy lawyer turned judge, a dull fellow who had written sonnets in his youth but now writes opinions; who describes himself as "useful but uninspiring, prosperous but prosaic." So the young wife runs off to Venice with the young artist—only to learn that the artist's mush is no better than the lawyer's mutton. Though I did not behave like either John or Augustin, the conflict between art and law was constantly pursuing me. My uncle Elkan Naumburg, who was horrified at the idea that a respectable young lawyer should write a play condoning adultery, tried to buy the entire edition to save me from what he foresaw as my inevitable ruin.

This desire to write plays as well as paint pictures continued to plague me. So much so that in 1927, a play called *Wall Street* was produced at the Hudson Theatre. Though friends hoped that the Hudson would be full to overflowing, the play was a failure. It deserved no better fate. I tried my hand again and again at play writing. But to no purpose.

That those exciting war years reached my palette is evidenced by a 1919 exhibition. Delmonico's Restaurant at Forty-fourth Street and Fifth Avenue became bankrupt in 1919. From a second-story balcony of the Delmonico Building, the Receiver and I, his lawyer, watched the march up Fifth Avenue of the victorious 27th Division, which had just returned to New York. During that thrilling day I made many pencil sketches, from which I produced twenty-eight small pastels. Mitchell Kennerley, owner of the then important Anderson Galleries—I find it hard to omit a vignette of that brilliant, mercurial, tragic figure, who was on Monday a devoted friend, on Tuesday an implacable foe—exhibited them at his galleries and published a book containing reproductions of them together with a critical note by C. Lewis Hind, from which I hope to demonstrate that I am justified in quoting:

> *"Has this artist conveyed the emotion he felt on that glorious March 25th when, through tears, we saw Fifth Avenue aflame with color and gazed at the tin helmets, keen khaki figures, just back from overseas and the grim business of war? The answer is yes. What he felt of color and movement he has communicated. . . . War passes. Art remains. It is something, indeed it is a triumph, to have created beauty, swift and sensitive, out of the banal brutality of war."*

Whether or not I deserved Hind's praise, it is his statement that I "communicated" which prompts me to ask whether contemporary avalanches of abstract paintings—the "atheism of art," Bernard Berenson calls them—"communicate." If not, is that because of the beholder's blindness? Or is it because many of today's so-called avant garde are not of today or tomorrow, but only yesteryear's rear guard, feeble

RETURN OF THE 27TH DIVISION: Pastel, 1919: Fogg
Art Museum, Harvard University, Cambridge, Massachusetts

RETURN OF THE 27TH DIVISION: Pastel, 1919: The artist

mimics of the revolutionary Picasso of a half century ago with nothing new to communicate?

Such questions have assailed me when looking at the tide of abstractions at recent Whitney Museum shows and at dealers' shops. I wonder what Gertrude Vanderbilt Whitney would think were she alive. Would she disagree with Berenson, whose 1953 book entitled *Seeing and Knowing* discusses man's need of art and declares that "it is not likely that he will henceforth be satisfied with the geometrical squares, lozenges, diagonals, circles, globes, trapezoids, parallelepidedons when he asks for the bread of art. . . . No perfection in smearing canvas guaranteed to represent nothing will replace pictures"?

Hind's emphasis on emotion as a wellspring of art furnishes my second reason for quoting him. Ecstasy, joy, love, fear, hate, Aristotelian pity and terror, the free play of fancy, the stuff that dreams and nightmares are made of, the sources of Picasso's magnificent, deeply moving Guernica, are as essential, I suggest, to creative visual art as they are to the poet; far more important than Euclid, for geometry is not art, and a mathematician is not a Titian (*vide* Mondrian).

LITHOGRAPHS

Where my etching efforts had been a dismal failure, it was a great day for me when in 1919 I was lucky enough to meet an able lithograph printer, George Miller. At his workshop on Fourteenth Street I made lithographs from time to time during the next ten years. The contrasts from blackest black to whitest white which the responsive lithographic stone encourages thrilled me. Bits of pumice, a pocketknife, a needle-sharp sort of small stiletto, sand rubbed on the stone, are only a few of the many varied means which reward the artist who diligently essays lithography and has the help of a master printer. Paper gets tired and worn. Not so the magical stone. Lithography was a great joy to me. I always meant to learn to become my own printer; from time to time I went to Miller's place. There, in October and November of 1929, I made my lithographs *Dies Irae, Madhouse,* and *The Shambles.*

AUCTION SALE

Through Mitchell Kennerley I came to know the amazing Alfred Stieglitz, husband of Georgia O'Keefe, champion of John Marin, Marsden Hartley, and other pioneers. When I occasionally visited Stieglitz he would hold me with his glittering eyes and pour forth torrents of brilliant talk until I fled exhausted. I wish I had had a tape recorder at those visits. I own three Marin watercolors which came from his establishment.

In 1919 Kennerley and Stieglitz cooked up the idea of persuading Hartley (who was cast to be a melancholy Dane) and me to hold a joint unrestricted auction sale of our pictures. One hundred and seventeen of the former's and seventy-five of mine were sold outright at the Anderson Galleries. The auction was like a first night at the theatre. Some of my clients and lawyer friends were there. To me the sale yielded barely enough to pay for the frames and the gallery charges. Hartley deservedly did a bit better. I still own two fine small early Hartleys which I bought there for about thirty dollars each.

In a letter to Kennerley printed in the sales catalogue I wrote:

> "An outright auction? Without reserve? What a humiliation if your pictures bring less than the cost of the frames! Thus an artist friend. . . . Humiliating? Nonsense. Ruysdael and Hobbema died in a poorhouse. Why wait for death and the dealer? I painted those pictures for the fun of it. I am selling them for the fun of it."

Painting in those days was indeed fun. My law practice prospered. I could pick and choose from the retainers offered me. I was a free man, law at day, art at night. We were half a mile from a deserted stretch of beach. On sunny Sundays we and our young children swam and cooked picnic lunches—never mind if they were too often garnished with sea sand. The U.S.A. was a wonderful place. Who guessed what the next quarter century had in store for mankind? Particularly what it portended for us Jews. Every picture I painted up to 1921 (except one of the 27th Division series which showed broken soldiers sitting on the curb opposite Delmonico's, crutches beside them) was more than fun. It was an explosion of my joy in nature. Sunshine or storm, winter or summer, tender greens and golds of spring, blaze of autumn, marshes or mountains, all were grist to my mill. Wordsworth was one of my teachers:

> ". . . The sounding cataract
> Haunted me like a passion; the tall rock
> The mountain . . . .
> Their colors and their forms . . ."

Was it he who said that remembered emotion is the poet's seed bed? I do not paint what I see but what I saw and felt and remember.

Not long after the end of World War I, Joseph Pennell gave a lithograph talk at the National Arts Club on Gramercy Park, of which long ago I became a life member. As a beginner with lithographs I was eager to hear what the celebrated Joe Pennell, whose nitric-acid tongue I had encountered in meetings with Rosenbach and Kennerley, had to say.

Denouncing artists who go to a printer's place and work directly on the lithographic stone, Pennell urged his artist audience to use lithographic pencils and transfer paper, as his master Whistler, said he, used to do. Thus, Pennell urged, the artist who leaves what he called the mere mechanical job of printing to a printer, can go forth into the world and make what he characterized as "honest, authentic lithographs."

George Bellows (with whom I played pool once or twice in the Club's basement) was in the audience. While I cannot quote Pennell verbatim, his talk closed with a vitriolic attack on Bellows, whose lithograph of the execution of the British nurse Edith Cavell by the Germans had attracted wide notice. "Had you used a lithographic pencil and paper and had the courage to risk going to Belgium instead of staying safely in the U.S.A.," Pennell exclaimed, "you might have made a true and honest picture directly from the scene."

Would Bellows answer this outrageous assault on his manhood as well as his art? There was a noticeable pause. We waited breathless. Bellows slowly rose to his feet. "I doubt whether the Kaiser would have issued a special invitation to me to witness the murder of Edith Cavell," he remarked at last. He paused. "But," he added, "that is not the point. The point is that Leonardo da Vinci was not a guest at the Last Supper." That was all. Bellows sat down.

For a few moments there was utter silence. Pennell

49

for once had no rejoinder. Thunderous applause followed. Rightly so. Bellows' retort was the epitome of the artist's function. Creation, not imitation. What a pity that George Bellows, one of our country's great artists, died so young.

2. ANOTHER WORLD

FELIX M. WARBURG

Luncheon with Felix M. Warburg at the Midday Club on Broad Street in July 1921 heralded an abrupt and vast change in my life. I surmised, of course, that an invitation from so busy and distinguished a man who knew me only slightly must have a purpose. I did not guess that I was about to be whisked into another world.

I had served as a director of the New York United Hebrew Charities under the leadership of Cyrus Sulzberger (father of Arthur) and Mortimer Schiff (Warburg's brother-in-law). I had been one of the founders of its successor, Jewish Federation, had also helped raise funds for the overseas work of JDC (American Jewish Joint Distribution Committee), headed by Mr. Warburg. But I knew nothing about its widespread activities, which began in 1914 when World War I laid a special toll on Jewish life in mid-Europe.

As I sipped my coffee wondering what Mr. Warburg had in mind, he remarked almost as casually as if talking about the weather—to this day I can quote him almost verbatim—"I am glad that you are willing to go abroad for a year as European head of JDC." "This," I managed to stammer after I had caught my breath, "is the first I have heard of any such suggestion. Why do you want me? What am I expected to do in Europe?" Though they were later to become as though carved into my skull, I even had to ask what those three letters "JDC" stood for.

The war was over; the time had come, Mr. Warburg explained, to close soup kitchens. "There must be economic rehabilitation. The Jews must not be pauperized. You have had a wide experience in reorganization. We want you to reorganize our European work, root and branch, and bring it into constructive channels." Dazed, I took his astounding proposal to Bessie.

Though her mother, born in Baltimore in 1862, was a deeply religious Jewess, Bessie's life was no more Jewish than was mine. Few of my clients were Jews. In art, theatre, trout fishing, and duck shooting, the question whether a man was a Jew had never arisen. Though we had joined a synagogue in Far Rockaway, I cannot recall that we ever crossed its threshold, except perhaps on Yom Kippur. What is this deep-rooted tie to the faith of our forefathers to which most of us cling, in face of or maybe because of centuries of persecution, even though our lives are remote from Judaism and its rituals?

Heedless of warnings that a year's absence from my law practice would be folly, I agreed to sail in October with Bessie, our children, and my indispensable secretary, Ruby Frisch (who has for forty years devotedly served me and all my family, and still does so, with undiminished fervor and good sense).

At once I plunged into studies of the problems which were to confront me. Cyrus Adler, Paul Baerwald. Herbert H. Lehman, Louis Marshall, and others, especially Mr. Warburg, were preceptors to an ignorant novice. Youthful, brilliant Lewis L. Strauss was helpful. Justice Louis D. Brandeis and Judge Julian W. Mack, ardent Zionists, urged the need of a cooperative agricultural bank in Palestine for the *Kibbutzim*. Mr. Warburg agreed. I was asked to help form the bank, and did so in London, chiefly through collaboration with the fascinating James de Rothschild, whom, to my regret, I never met again. The bank has served and still serves great and ever growing purposes in Israel.

Those months of preparation taught me at least one thing which I have never forgotten. Deep and wide as were (and are) the schisms which split apart my stiff-necked fellow Jews, bitterly as Zionists and anti-Zionists, orthodox and reform Jews, labor leaders and management may oppose one another, our determination to help our fellow Jews in need was and is an unbreakable bond among nearly all of us. It was an inspiring lesson to learn.

In August of that, to me, fateful year of 1921, Russia, suffering from a famine which threatened the lives of many millions, appealed for help to Herbert Hoover, then head of the ARA (American Relief Administration). Mr. Hoover, who was then also head of the U.S. Department of Commerce, convened a meeting in Washington of Red Cross, Y.M.C.A., Y.W.C.A., Quakers, Knights of Columbus, and other leading organizations including JDC, which I attended with Mr. Warburg and Lewis L. Strauss. This led later to the biggest undertaking of my life —an undertaking which had a tragic end. Though it has nothing directly to do with art, I will have to outline it in due course because of its deep and lasting effect upon me and my pictures.

Were this a JDC story I would be telling about Jewish leaders and all sorts of groups I met in various lands; about the Vienna riots of November 1921 when kronen vanished almost to zero and Communists tried to take over Austria; about my 1921 midwinter visit to typhus-ridden Poland, most of whose three million Jews Hitler later obliterated; about my JDC reorganization efforts. There would have been many pages. But this is meant to be an art book even if my story must at times leap from my studio to events which entered into my pictures.

At the JDC European head office in Paris I received a visit one day from Sholom Asch (whose recent death I mourn). Working together for the Jews of Poland, we struck up what became a lasting friendship. I did a rapid pastel sketch of his sorrowful profile. At the Dôme Restaurant on the Left Bank, Asch had me meet the painter, Moise Kisling, who brought me to Zborowski, dealer in and owner of most of the works of the then recently deceased Italian Jew, Modigliani.

Kisling and the sculptor Lipchitz had made a death mask of Modigliani's beautiful face. Kisling gave it to me because it made him unhappy to look at it. I presented it to the Fogg Museum, had several bronze replicas made, one of which is in our 67th Street home; another I gave to the Museum of Modern Art.

Modigliani overwhelmed me. From Zborowski I bought a dozen or more of his oils for about two hundred dollars each; also *Caryatids* and small drawings. Kisling also took me to Soutine, whose studio was a hovel. I could probably have bought every canvas he owned for a few francs. They did not then "communicate" to me. I was blind, as perhaps I am today in assailing much of contemporary abstract art.

Asch, who knew painters and writers, used to call for

me now and then late in the afternoon at my JDC office on Rue Lyautey in Passy and take me to the Left Bank. We were invariably escorted or followed by two mysterious fellows, spies on or protectors of Asch. We never discovered who they were or what their business was.

Asch and I planned to visit Picasso, Matisse, and other artists. We particularly wanted to call on Gertrude Stein (who, like me, was born in 1874 in Allegheny City, Pa.). These plans unfortunately came to nothing. Asch left Paris and I was hard at work; for, as Gertrude might have said, "A job is a job is a job is a job." And so my nose was kept to the grindstone in efforts to serve the Jews of Central Europe, Palestine, and Russia.

Years later, when Hitler conquered France, I managed to help Kisling get to the United States. I have a lovely flower piece which he presented to me. I saw a Kisling recently at a dealer's shop on Fifty-seventh Street. He asked $3,000 for it. That might have pleased Kisling, who never won the recognition which I believe he well deserves.

On free afternoons I left my busy JDC office at Passy and with Kisling or Asch visited dealers' shops. I met painters at the Dôme, the Alphabet, and Rotonde restaurants. I bought the famous *Jeune Marin* by Matisse for $500; paintings by Derain, Van Dongen, Vlaminck, Pascin, Dufy, Signac, Medgyes, Kisling, Zadkine, a small *montage* by Picasso; also works of two Russian refugees, Gregoriev and Soudeikin. In all, I invested a bit more than $5,000 for a collection which would now be worth a fortune. Of all those treasures I own only one Modigliani and a couple of Gregorievs. I gave my sister Minnie a lovely Signac water color which she generously gave back to me. It is now in the collection of the Fogg Museum of Art.

A Paris spring evening in 1922 explains what became of my treasures (which today would fetch almost enough for a king's ransom). My hale and hearty uncle, Max Naumburg, and his handsome, witty wife, Therese, had Bess and me dine with them at the Voltaire Restaurant. Aged seventy, my uncle had wound up his clothing business. He loved pictures. My aunt, who always got her way, demanded that I find something to occupy him.

Why not start an art gallery in New York? Why not show unknown artists like Modigliani; also gifted young Americans? Such thoughts having flashed through my mind, I offered my uncle the pictures I had bought for myself plus $3,000, provided that he and his brother Aaron would each put in an equal $8,000. Twenty-four thousand dollars of capital, we thought, should suffice to run a gallery for a few years, give us some fun, and might introduce unknown talent to the American art market.

When my overseas service ended, Bessie and I had a vacation trip in England. At King Arthur's Castle, a hostelry at Tintagel, I wrote a fantastic ballet called *Punchinello*. It was published by Mitchell Kennerley. It seeks to express things which Europe had put into my mind. One may look in vain for the word "Jew" in that little book, but its protagonist's hook nose and hump are symbols. A painter friend whom I had met in Paris—Ladislas Medgyes—produced it at a little theatre on the Left Bank. I was not there to see it.

In November 1922 the New Gallery, financed by my two uncles and myself, opened its doors at 606 Madison Avenue. It was an immediate success. I wrote for our opening:

> *"Though we shall show the works of those who have arrived, we wish in the main to be explorers . . . In Paris*

the 'amateur' is the collector who buys the picture he loves. He hangs them on his walls and draws daily dividends of pleasure. Forty years ago he bought Manet and Monet; twenty years ago Cézanne, Gauguin, and Van Gogh. He enjoys the sensation of having backed his own judgment . . . of making it possible for the artist to live, to create and gain recognition."

Our first exhibition included five large Modigliani *Caryatid* drawings, for which I had paid Zborowski $100 apiece. They were snatched up at $250 each. Today, I am told, they fetch up to $10,000 or more. When the $500 Matisse *Jeune Marin* brought $1,000, we threw our hats in the air. We thought ourselves super salesmen. Theodore Rousseau of the Metropolitan Museum has told me that some years ago it fetched $38,-000. Not all my purchases were financially so lucky. The Russians, Gregoriev and Soudeikin, seem to have been forgotten.

The catalogue of a show which soon followed priced five Matisse oils from $500 to $750 each; the Dufys at $300 each; the Modigliani *Caryatids* at $200; Modigliani oils, *La Reveuse*, $600, *Portrait of M.M.C.*, $600, *Tête de Femme*, $600. There were three Vlaminck *aquarelles* at $250 each. Nearly all of those Paris purchases of mine were quickly snapped up. Only one favorite Modigliani, for which I had paid Zborowski $250, I kept for myself. It is a portrait of Jeanne Hebuterne. I have refused $30,000 for it. But I was sorely tempted to let it go. What a lot of pictures by unknown artists I could buy with such a nest egg!

In 1923, the New Gallery published a book consisting mainly of reproductions of pictures; fifty-eight of these sold during our first season. Its foreword said:

> *"Ever since the great Armory Show of 1913, the pathfinders have had an audience, small though it is, and it is primarily for this audience that this book has been prepared."*

Small audience? Today the Coliseum could not hold collectors if they hoped to acquire a Modigliani oil for $600 or even for $6,000.

A Woodstock exhibition opened our second season. "Yes, we have no Rembrandts. But we have Woodstock," our catalogue boasted. "We regard the pictures here shown as some of the best of contemporary art. America needs its artists as much as its artists need America. Don't just murmur 'How interesting.' Ask: 'How much?'" Of the Woodstock artists we selected thirty-four years ago, it is worthwhile to list a few:

Peggy Bacon	Marsden Hartley
George Bellows	Robert Henri
George Biddle	Georgina Klitgaard
Arnold Blanch	John Marin
Alexander Brook	Henry Mattson
Ernest Fiene	Henry L. McFee
Harry Gottlieb	Hermon More

The two paintings by Hermon More, now director of the Whitney Museum, were entitled *Group of Houses, Eddyville, N.Y.* and *Factory Town* (each priced at $300). They were not, if my recollection serves me, abstractions.

In 1924 my uncle wearied of the New Gallery. I induced George S. Hellman, a college mate of my youth, to run it. He did it so successfully that it ceased to be an adventure. JDC, law, and painting filled my life. The New Gallery closed its doors. I venture the hope that its brief life span not only introduced Modigliani to this country, but also helped American artists to gain recognition.

Our return from Europe to Far Rockaway in 1922 was not a happy one. An enterprising neighbor, who had seemed to be a friend and who had formed and was president of the "Far Rockaway Beautiful Association," had surrounded our home with little tapestry brick houses which he built on bits of land and which were squares on a checkerboard. For a year we lived at Far Rockaway imprisoned by those houses and their occupants. Then we fled and found nine acres with a fishpond, in Scarsdale. That has since then been our home. Here our children grew up; married; reared their families. But our home is not quite empty, for here children and grandchildren are often with us.

Years ago I revisited the Far Rockaway home of our youth. Our flower gardens and lilac hedge were tangled masses of burdock, ragweed, and thistles. The house had been demolished. Only the brick chimney of my studio, broken and blackened, remained to recall those early happy years. I never went there again. Today our Scarsdale acres are surrounded by ranch houses, but we do not see them. In 1923 I planted a thousand six-inch pine trees. They have become a green fortress.

SHANTY BROOK

In 1923 Howard and Ann Reber, Philadelphia friends, had Bessie and me visit them at their Elizabethtown summer camp. On the shoulder of Mount Hurricane, overlooking that little Adirondack village on which I had first set eyes in 1887, Reber showed us the Ryan 254-acre abandoned farm. We bought it but nearly lost it when Ryan excluded twenty-nine acres from the purchase (insisting that they were not in the deal). Daumier could have painted, or Dickens could have described, the night scene in lawyer Dudley's office when we quarreled till midnight about those twenty-nine acres through which coursed the best stretch of trout water on Falls Brook.

Through those wooded hills sparkled little Shanty Brook, from which my son Robert, at the age of four, caught his first trout.

From our acres we could see Mount Cobble, Giant, Hurricane, and on clear days even Vermont's Green Mountains, blue, not green, in the far distance. Bessie and I tramped up and down those acres to select a building site. In the camp which Livingston Woodruff built, in accordance with plans drawn by Bessie and me, we and our three children spent happy summers. Now that they are married they and their spouses and their children love Shanty Brook nearly as much as we do. There in the Adirondacks, with their ever changing moods, I find the chief sources for my landscapes. There I escape from a grim world; there my painting, trout fishing, and (with my most prized possession, a bulldozer) building ever more and ever more dams and pools for ever more trout, fill my days.

To the west, Hurricane Mountain lifts its classic peak toward the setting sun. To see it from our camp porch we had to cut down a small forest of towering white pines which gave us a year's logs for our fireplaces. That mountain means as much to me, I believe, as did Mont Sainte Victoire to Paul Cézanne, but I have never painted a Mount Hurricane picture which satisfied me.

Every spring comes the May and June trout fishing. Shanty Brook, Falls Brook, and Jackson Brook join forces at the foot of our acres. There I have built a series of trout pools for wary *salvelinus fontinalis*. The list of my fishing companions over these past more than three decades would be a long one. Henry L. Stimson, whom I first met when he was a young United States attorney and I was trying to put crooked bankrupts behind the bars, used to come fishing with me from the Ausable Club. He was very weary the last time he fished with me and came up to my camp for a rest. I laid a few birch logs on the fire while he stretched himself at length on the big couch near the blaze. Somehow I happened to have a bottle of Rheims champagne in my icebox. He had only recently returned from a mission to that historic city. The champagne seemed to make a new man of him. When he said good-by, he promised to fish with me soon again. Death prevented him from keeping his promise. He was one of our country's great men.

AGROJOINT

Agrojoint (American Jewish Joint Agricultural Corporation) is the story of what grew out of the Hoover 1921 Russian famine relief. It has nothing to do with art, but so much with my life, that an outline is necessary.

A trained agronomist was needed to help plant 1922 and 1923 Soviet crops designed to resist drought and rescue Russia from a second-year famine. The resourceful Warburg found a Russian-born American, a famous agronomist named Joseph A. Rosen, who became a leading member of the Hoover mission to Russia. Rosen not only performed miracles, but also, familiar with the fertile soil of the Crimea, which for lack of water was sparsely inhabited, brought a few American Keystone drillers to that region, found abundant underground waters, and by 1923 settled a few hundred Russian ghetto Jews on that rich vacant Crimean soil.

Never before farmers, they nevertheless did very well. (We wandering Jews adapt ourselves. We have had to.) Thereupon in 1924 the watchful Soviet authorities, in dire need of vast crop increase, suggested an extensive Jewish farm settlement in the Crimea. This gave JDC a chance to free many of the two million Russian Jews from the ghettos of Russia. JDC had me form Agrojoint, put Rosen and me at its head, and provided ample funds for large scale Crimean work.

When by 1926 Rosen had performed the unbelievable achievement of transforming over fifty thousand Jews into hardy, productive Crimean farmers, the Soviet Union asked for consultations looking to a far larger expansion of our work. Thereupon JDC asked me to go to Russia with Dr. Bernhard Kahn (who had succeeded me as JDC European head) to meet Dr. Rosen and the Soviet authorities.

Early spring of 1926 thus found Bessie and me in Italy for a vacation trip prior to my journey to Russia. Traveling from Naples, to Rome, to Florence, our eyes for the first time feasted on the treasures of the Uffizi and Pitti, of Orvieto, Perugia, Assisi, and Siena. I acquired a fine copy of Botticelli's *Primavera,* which was painted by an art student in Florence. It adorns my city home at Sixty-seventh Street and gives me immense pleasure. What poet has better expressed springtime, youth, beauty, and a world of peace and joy?

While we were in Rome an old foreign woman attempted to assassinate Mussolini. "Jews," cried the Fascisti, and mobbed old bearded Hebrews. This led to my writing a poem on the very large menu of the Ulpia Restaurant—once a basilica—where Bessie and I had a copious luncheon. Twenty years later I found that poem among some papers in my studio. In 1947 it was published in the *Menorah Journal,* whose editor,

Henry Hurwitz, has consented to its publication in this book. That poem being as revealing a part of me as anything in my entire life, I include it as a sort of epilogue. It is an overture to the somber paintings of my late years.

BERLIN

In Berlin on the way to Russia I met Dr. Kahn and planted a rosebush in his garden. A Jewish rosebush? Did Hitler destroy it? A dinner party was given for me at the splendid Wahnsee home of Lola Hahn, glamorous daughter of Felix Warburg's banker brother Max. There I met some twenty topmost German Jews who were eager to know about the Crimean work. Albert Einstein was one of the guests.

When the time came for me to speak, I dealt but briefly with the Crimea and turned to another topic. This, be it remembered, was 1926. Taking a magazine called *Bren Essel* (Nettle) from my pocket, I told how by chance I had picked up that savage anti-Semitic journal at the Berlin railway station. Pointing to hideously offensive caricatures of some of the very men who sat at that dinner table and to inciting libels against them, I asked what was being done to stop Hitler. They listened tolerantly to this ignorant American and assured him that Hitler was just another one of those harmless demagogues who from time to time rose briefly to the surface and soon vanished. Germany, they told me, suffered no such anti-Semitism as did we of the U.S.A. They were members of some of Germany's most exclusive clubs. Einstein's warnings were heeded no more than were mine. Who can blame them?

That never-forgotten dinner meeting prompted a

pastel sketch made in a fury as soon as I got back to the United States. It is reproduced in black and white in this book. I intended it as a basis for a large painting to be called *History of the Jews.* I have never had the heart to make it. Anyway, the death of Hitler shows that it is not the whole history. Not by a jugful.

U. S. S. R.

From Berlin I proceeded with Kahn and my secretary, Ruby Frisch, to Moscow. On May 1, Rosen met us at the Moscow railway station and hurried us to choice seats at the Red Square. There I was not more than fifty feet from Stalin, who stood on the tomb of Lenin reviewing the parade. He wore a sort of chauffeur's cap and looked like a struggling taxi driver. I did not comprehend his malignant power.

The next day we met with Smidovich, the cooperative, intelligent Vice-President of the Soviet Union. He was head of "Komzet," which had charge of the U.S.S.R. relations with our Crimean work. We soon concluded a pact with him whereby Russia placed vast Crimea lands, forests, and lumber, and funds up to ten million dollars, at our entire disposal for great enlargement of the Crimean work. The pact also offered Soviet government bonds to us for another ten million dollars, which we were asked not to give, but to lend to the Soviet state for our work under Rosen's direction. We all expected that in twenty years we would settle over a million self-supporting Jewish farmers on the rich Crimean soil. From Moscow we went to the Crimea, where I was overjoyed by the successes of our settlers, and their fields, farms, homes, and villages.

Thence I journeyed to Le Touquet, in France, where I had lunch with Julius Rosenwald, who had backed this work since 1921. He listened closely to my story. When I paused for breath he quietly pledged two million toward the ten for the Crimean work. He was a man of few words and big deeds.

After my return to the United States, I went to Washington and reported to Mr. Hoover, who thereupon wrote me describing the Crimean work as "one of the outstanding pieces of human engineering in the world." His letter helped toward the raising of the ten-million-dollar loan. John D. Rockefeller also helped by giving us half a million dollars, writing me that the Crimea work was a "notable and creative example of social engineering." When Mr. Rosenwald and I lunched with Mr. Warburg at the Kuhn, Loeb dining room at 52 William Street, Mr. Warburg provided a million dollars toward the ten, whereupon Mr. Rosenwald raised his share to five millions, declined Mr. Warburg's car, said good-by, and went uptown by subway to a Sears, Roebuck conference. It was the last time I ever met him. In 1927 my lifelong friend Alfred A. Knopf published my account of the Crimean undertaking. The title of my book was *On the Steppes.*

In 1938, when more than three hundred thousand self-supporting Jews were tilling millions of fertile Crimean acres and raising families as well as foodstuffs, Hitler was on the rampage. War was in the air. Suddenly Stalin called a halt to our work. Rosen and our small staff had to come home. Our plans, hopes, and dreams were forced to an abrupt end. War came. The Crimea, a haven remote, we had believed, from the clash of arms (study the map), was overrun by Hitler's hordes. Our settlers were mowed down. The few who escaped Hitler's murderous fury have vanished. Was Stalin an anti-Semite? Did he complete Hitler's murders? Never a single message from a survivor has come to us. When I was in Israel in 1950 I met one of our Crimean farmers; he had miraculously escaped to Israel. He knew of no others. Thus ended in ashes, ruin, and death the greatest work of Rosen's life and mine. Does anyone need to ask whether such events leave a painter untouched?

FOGG ART MUSEUM

It is a relief to turn to a happy event. My trips with Bessie to visit her family in Boston gave me opportunities to go to the Fogg Museum, at Harvard, in the creation of which Felix Warburg had a major part. There I hobnobbed with Paul J. Sachs, who encouraged me to paint—especially by accepting a few of my pictures for the Fogg Museum and by showing my lithographs there—attended lectures, met curators and students, and noted the rapid growth of the Museum from year to year.

My uncle Aaron Naumburg (whose help in financing the New Gallery I have mentioned) was a successful merchant. He had begun in the early part of this century to collect American paintings. Chiefly I recall his Bruce Crane and J. Francis Murphy landscapes. By 1920 all the Americans had vanished. Step by step, paintings by Rembrandt, Rubens, Hals, Murillo, El Greco, and a few other great works made up my uncle's and aunt's superb small collection. How they came to choose so wisely I never learned. It was housed at their home—1 West Sixty-seventh Street—almost next door to my apartment at number 27. Thus I saw much of my aunt and uncle and their gradual acquisitions of treasures.

When in the spring of 1928 my aunt and uncle told me that they intended their collection to go to a museum after their deaths and asked for my suggestions, I daringly proposed that they move their entire Naumburg Room and its contents to the Fogg Art Museum. The idea caught fire even though it involved the heavy cost of building a wing for the Museum.

As they were about to go to Europe, my uncle had me draw a will whereby he bequeathed the collection to his wife. This, he said, would serve until their return to New York. A few weeks later he died suddenly at Monte Catini in Italy. For many months my aunt was prostrated; but in 1929 she consented to have me arrange for Paul J. Sachs and his colleague, Edward Forbes, to visit her. The visit led to correspondence and many discussions; finally to a return visit by my aunt and me to the Fogg Museum during the 1929 Christmas season. The decision she then reached was expressed in great detail in the will she had me draft for her as soon as we returned to New York. Only a few weeks after she signed it, she too died as suddenly as had my uncle. *Streptococcus viridans* (now, I believe, readily conquerable by sulfa or penicillin or one or more of the wonder drugs of our time) suddenly snuffed out her life.

What had happened while she lived and what took place after her death can be gathered from the dedication exercises on November 9, 1932, of the Naumburg wing of the Fogg Art Museum. The President of Harvard, A. Lawrence Lowell, who delivered an address of thanks, called on me to respond. Here are a few words only of what I had prepared and said during those dark days of depression:

> *"Here within these tranquil academic walls is the room which Aaron Naumburg and Nettie Goldsmith Naumburg, his wife, transported to this shelter from the alarms of a*

dark and frightened world to this great college, this island of youth.

"Today this room is dedicated to youth and will carry into distant corners of a drab world the vision which created Fogg and which created this room; these fragile bits of canvas and pigment, the flowerings of poets' and painters' dreams; these, if naught else, are perennius aere, *lanterns in a world which the vaunted skill of economist, statesman and lawyer, of scientist and soldier have only darkened."*

The list of Fogg students who have become leading figures and educators in the field of art would make a grand book. Our countrymen owe much to Sachs and Forbes and their successors and disciples, and to Fogg's present able director, John Coolidge; and though now in this nuclear era of guided missiles the cry is for education of scientists, I know that at Fogg the lessons of art, speaking a perennial and universal language of peace, are winning many pupils.

On November 8, 1957, at the invitation of John Coolidge, I went to Fogg Art Museum to take part in the twenty-fifth anniversary celebration of the dedication of the Naumburg Room. When I walked into John Coolidge's office a few minutes before the ceremonies took place, he handed me a document showing that my pictures are not in the cellar of Fogg Museum but are scattered through several important Harvard buildings. When he and I walked together from his office to the Naumburg Room, there, at its entrance, were two of my pastels of 1919—"Return of the Twenty-Seventh Division"—which I had not seen for thirty-eight years.

In 1929 Louis Marshall (President of the American Jewish Committee), Felix M. Warburg (head of JDC), Chaim Weizmann (leader of the Zionists), convened a meeting at Zurich of some four hundred or more Zionist and non-Zionist Jewish leaders from all parts of the world. The purpose was to create a Jewish Agency through which all who wished to help the sound growth of Jewish life in Palestine might collaborate. There I submitted a resolution, unanimously adopted, which contained no suggestion for the creation of a Jewish state, since we, the non-Zionists, were determined to exclude any political ideas and did not support creation of a Jewish sovereign state. What it did contain was a sincere offer of full Jewish collaboration with Arabs toward the building of a good life in Palestine for Jew and Arab alike. In immediate response to this olive branch from world Jewry, Arabs at once committed wholesale murders of Palestinian Jews.

It was by Marshall's appointment—I had been a sort of lieutenant for him—that I had been made chairman of the Resolutions Committee. I loved and revered Marshall, a great lawyer, a great Jew, a great citizen of the U.S.A. During the long Zurich sessions his energy, patience, and wisdom were a powerful factor toward welding together nearly all factions of Jewry for help in Palestine. Scarcely did the meeting come to an end when sudden death took him from us.

DEPRESSION

No sooner had I re-entered my office in September of 1929 than I found an urgent message from Edwin A. Potter to get in touch with him. He was a vice-president of Guaranty Trust Company, a long-time friend and client with whom I not only fished for trout and salmon, but also, in 1919, had made a "killing." At once I looked him up. Stocks, he said, were dangerously high. He urged me to sell many of the securities in which I had invested and to get myself wholly out of debt. It was a lucky thing for me that I did get myself out of debt.

I had thought myself wealthy. On paper I had been rich. It had been a pleasant fantasy. The financial cyclones which struck in October and November hit me hard. I returned to the law at full speed, and was called into many of the large bankruptcy and reorganization cases which the depression brought on.

In the afternoon of October 28, 1929, the terrible day when nine million shares were slaughtered on the New York Stock Exchange, I rushed to Miller's place and made my lithograph *Dies Irae*. On the horrible November 13 seven-million-share day, I escaped again from the Wall Street inferno and made another which I called *The Shambles,* of which there is only one impression. It is owned by the Metropolitan Museum. These were the overtures to my later "Ironism" and "Atomism" pictures of a world in chaos.

Those October and November nightmares which heralded world depression and war contain a grim warning. From September to December 1929, security market values tumbled from the sky to the sub-cellar. In November the Stock Exchange closed its doors. Dull financial statistics cannot portray the ruin which befell countless thousands of men and women who in September carried stocks on margin and counted themselves rich, and who on Christmas Day were bankrupts. Those fearful days and nights of world-wide ruin which presaged World War II inevitably reached my palette.

Kreuger, the match king, the collapse of his world-

DIES IRAE: Lithograph, 1929: New York Public Library

THE SHAMBLES: Lithograph, 1929: Metropolitan Museum of Art, New York

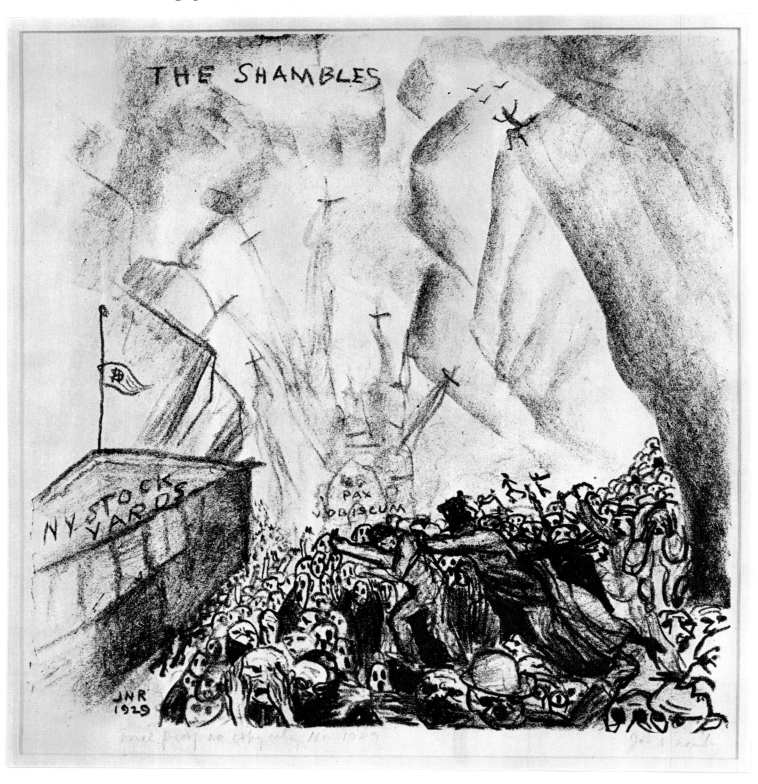

MADHOUSE: Lithograph, 1929: Museum of Fine Arts, Boston, Massachusetts

wide empire built upon matches, and the resulting bankruptcy of International Match Company brought the peak of my work as a bankruptcy lawyer. For five years much of my energy went to unwinding the match tangle and working day and night to rebuild shattered businesses. Meantime Hitler and his agents were busily spreading anti-Semitism throughout this country, which dragged me into continuous extralegal activities reflected in my later paintings.

LEAGUE OF NATIONS AND WORLD PEACE

One of these activities resulted when, following a meeting at my home, in 1933 Mr. Warburg brought about the appointment of a co-worker, our tried friend and true, James G. McDonald, as League of Nations High Commissioner for Refugees. For two years McDonald struggled with might and main to find asylum for German Jews and "non-Aryans" whom Hitler was destroying. Neither the League nor the world's nations gave McDonald anything better than empty lip service.

In 1935 he revisited me. His thatch of yellow hair had turned to silver. He told me that the only course open to him was to resign his office. We decided that a powerful letter of resignation might focus the world's attention not only on Hitler's destruction of Jews but on the Nazi threat of world war. The McDonald letter of resignation, in the preparation of which Mr. Warburg, Morris R. Cohen, S. J. Stroock, Oscar Janowsky, Melvin Fagen, and Norman Bentwich collaborated with McDonald and with me, was published in December, 1935, and reached the press of the world during the peace-on-earth Christmas season. It set forth Hitler's "Master Race" concept, his cruel Nuremberg laws and his fearful persecutions, reviewed many precedents of international law, called for "firm intercession" by the League and the nations of the world and reached its climax in a solemn warning that Hitler's acts constituted a grave danger to international peace. It fell on deaf ears of a world which found fault with President Roosevelt's "quarantine" address and preferred to appease Hitler.

At our instance world leaders then handed the League a petition stating that:

> "The undersigned, representing many religious faiths, political views and nationalities, call upon the League of Nations to take action in defense of those elementary human rights which are the very foundation stones of civilization and which constitute a primary condition of continued international peace and good will."

Again the League paid no heed. Thereby it sounded its death knell. It will be well for the United Nations and its delegates to take those facts to heart.

Our third and last effort to rouse world conscience was a book written at the instance of Morris R. Cohen and me by two able scholars, Oscar Janowsky and Melvin Fagen, entitled *International Aspects of German Racial Policies*. It was published in 1937 by the Oxford Press. The opening paragraph of an introduction written by Cohen and me asks questions not yet answered by the world:

> "Is national sovereignty so absolute that a government may without limit oppress or even destroy whole groups of its citizens; Have other states no rights or duty to protest or intercede? . . . What is the civilized world to do when a nation makes persecution of its minorities a matter of declared governmental policy? These are the basic issues which this book examines in the light of international practice during the past three centuries."

A significant forward step was the 1948 adoption, by the United Nations, of the Genocide Convention—something in which I had part as chairman of a committee organized by the National Conference of Christians and Jews. That promise of the world's nations, together with the U.N. Declaration of Human Rights accomplished largely through the magnificent labors of Eleanor Roosevelt, represents historic attempts to introduce into the field of international law those principles of equal human rights for which mankind must still struggle. Up to now these ideals have only too often been mere scraps of paper. When will the United Nations square its deeds with its charter? What of the 1949 armistice agreement brought about by it between Egypt and Israel which both nations accepted as an indispensable step toward the restoration of peace, in the face of which Egypt still holds on to its belligerent rights? What about the Suez Canal and Hungary? Has the world forgotten Chamberlain's appeasement of Hitler through which he boasted he had accomplished "peace in our time"? And is it to be expected that such events can be driven out of my head and heart when I slam the door of my studio on the world?

Grenville Clark here appropriately re-enters my story. His considerate conduct toward me, long ago, led to our durable friendship. When he was writing his great treatise, recently published by the Harvard University Press, I happened to suggest a title for it. Clark has reminded me of what I had long forgotten, and has presented me with a copy of *World Peace Through World Law*. This admirable blue print for revision of the United Nations charter blazes the path toward the kind of world mankind craves.

Have I wandered from the happy field of art? If so, I turn to a memorable evening in 1936 when Bessie and I dined with Alfred and Blanche Knopf at their house on Purchase Street in the Westchester town of Harrison—a property I had found for them long ago. After one of their Lucullan feasts Alfred gave me one of the many Borzoi publications with which he has showered me for years. It was the Gerstle Mack biography of Paul Cézanne.

While I had for twenty years studied and revered the master's works, the Mack book gave me a new insight into Cézanne's credo as repeatedly emphasized in his many letters; particularly those to the painters Camoin and Bernard. To enter at length into Cézanne's credo is beyond the province of this book. But so profound has been his influence on me and so widespread are the misconceptions of his aesthetic that I must quote at least a few lines from those famous letters.

> *"I go ahead very slowly as nature appears very complex." "The artist must avoid the literary spirit which so often leads the painter astray from his real mission, the concrete study of nature." "One cannot be too scrupulous, too sincere or too humble before nature." "I seek the realization of that part of nature, which coming into our view gives us the picture." "The idea to be insisted upon is . . . to produce the image of what we see." "I simply must produce after nature."*

On September 21, 1906, a month before his death, the sick, old man wrote the last of his letters to Bernard. He is still going on with his "researches"; is *"continually making observations from nature . . . you will forgive me for harping continually on the same string."* Five days later he wrote his son, *"I am still working from nature on the banks of the Arc."*

Continuing his "researches" for the last time, on October 15 he climbs across a hilly country to work at his "motif"; paints until drenched to the skin by a violent rainstorm; struggles homeward; collapses at the roadside; is brought home by the driver of a laundry cart; a week later breathes his last.

As to Cézanne's endless studies of the object before him, he required one hundred and fifteen sittings for his celebrated Vollard portrait. When the weary Vollard moved his head a few inches, Cézanne angrily demanded that he *"sit still like an apple."* After the last sitting the master merely remarked that he was not *"displeased with the shirt front."*

In 1951, a leading spokesman for modern art wrote in an important museum publication that "Cézanne practically negated the significance of all representational subject matter." He further insisted that the "legacy passed on" by the master was to "the cubists and through them to the geometrical abstractionists." I confess I find it impossible in face of the Cézanne letters and paintings to understand such a point of view.

Cézanne's first letter to Bernard, written on April 15, 1904, perhaps gives us at least a clue to such misconceptions. This was the famous "cylinder, sphere, cone" missive. It said nothing about cubes. What it said was that *"you must see in nature the cylinder, the sphere, the cone."* Have the art experts overlooked or refused to heed Cézanne's emphasis on nature?

Years earlier Monet had opened my eyes to nature's radiant garments; now Cézanne showed me her very heart and skeleton; it has been those depths that I have sought, and seek, to penetrate.

Carried away, as have been hosts of other painters, by tidal waves of recent and current abstract art and its powerful champions, and by the apparent belief that Cézanne was Picasso's progenitor, I tried to paint abstractions. I destroyed them. It is not in me to negate or forsake nature. Even so bold a modernist as Matisse wrote, in 1948, "*An artist must possess nature . . . must become one with nature.*" Cézanne has given me courage steadfastly to blaze my own trail wherever it may lead. Landscape painting, which is my chief preoccupation, is not in the present fashion. What of it? There is nothing fashionable about sunrises or storms or mountains.

This disquisition needs a few final words about Picasso, who in 1923 approved a statement prepared by him with the help of Marius de Zayas, translated into English, and then published in ARTS (edited by Forbes Watson) as Picasso's own credo. Its opening gun was his declaration that "*I can hardly understand the importance given to the word 'research' in connection with modern painting.*" Did Picasso refer to Cézanne? If not, to whom else? Squarely challenging Cézanne's oft expressed devotion to nature, Picasso became even more outspoken. "*Nature and art being two different things,*" he insisted, "*cannot be the same thing. Through art we express our conception of what nature is not.*"

Perhaps it would be worth while for the experts to take a new look at these two towering figures. Were they, aesthetically speaking, father and son? If so, did not the son repudiate the parent? Contrast Cézanne's magnificent *Bathers* at the Philadelphia Museum with Picasso's *Demoiselles d'Avignon,* (which experts have said was inspired by Cézanne's *Bathers*), and judge for yourself. Read Gerstle Mack's book or Cézanne's letters translated into English and edited by John Rewald, published in 1941 in London by Bruno Cassirer.

Early in October 1937 I lunched at 52 William Street with Felix Warburg for the last time. He had just returned from an exhausting trip to Europe to find a way of something like peace for the Jews of Palestine, who were then pawns of British imperial policy.

It was the last of his innumerable services to mankind —not alone for his fellow Jews but in endless directions which moved his keen mind and great heart. His face was grayish-white and drawn. His lips were pale. His cheeks were deep valleys. His dark eyes seemed to have sunk into his skull. When I could not help expressing concern about his health, that irresistible smile of his lighted his wan face. Remarking that "the best definition of a bore is a man, who, when asked how he feels, tells you," he brushed aside my questions and turned the talk to his plan to create cantons in Palestine somewhat as in Switzerland, so as to give at least a shred of autonomy to a canton for Palestinian Jews. So deep was his faith in human beings that he refused to believe that friendship of Arabs could not be won.

On October 20, 1937, the man who had altered and enlarged the dimensions of my life died. On my seventy-fifth birthday, his widow Frieda gave me his silver bedside clock.

WORLD WAR II

When we entered World War I, I had been young enough to try to do my bit. When Pearl Harbor plunged us into another war I was approaching my seventieth year. For some months I struggled to practice law, but in 1942 I retired from the law firm I had headed for thirty years. I became its counsel, but dropped all legal matters except for those cases in which I owed a personal duty to clients. Meantime I devoted myself to fighting Hitlerism so far as I could do so.

Russia being our ally, I joined the Board of Russian War Relief at the invitation of the late Allen Wardwell. That nation-wide organization sent millions of dollars of foodstuffs, clothing, and medicaments to the people of the Soviet Union.

Stalin's Order of the Day issued May 1, 1942, published in the U.S.A. in a handsome brochure, lured us to the belief that our contributions to Russia would help toward durable friendship and peace with the U.S.S.R. "First place among freedom-loving countries is held by Great Britain and the United States to which we are bound by ties of friendship and alliance," wrote Stalin. "We do not set ourselves the aim of seizing foreign countries. . . . We want to liberate our brothers, the Ukrainians, Moldavians, Lithuanians, Letts, Estonians and Karelians." Can we blame President Eisenhower and John Foster Dulles for their discounting of the Soviet's peaceful protestations today?

A visit to my native city of Pittsburgh in 1942 in behalf of Russian War Relief started me on a series of pictures exhibited in 1944 at the Ferargil Gallery in New York. The title of my show was "Ironism." Several of these pictures are reproduced in this book; one pastel particularly, dated 1944 but which I began to work at in 1942, while Hitler was at the peak of his power, bears the title, *Is This the Man Who Makes the Earth to Tremble?* Whether or not it has merit, it seems to have been prophetic. For the catalogue I wrote a foreword from which I quote a paragraph, believing it to have contemporary meaning:

> "With awe I beheld Pittsburgh's plumes of smoke and steam, her chimneys, totem poles and fortresses. Here at my

birthplace flourished the arsenal of democracy; here was America. Iron, which was to be man's servant, became his master. The ploughshare was beaten into tanks. To this plight has man's genius brought man. Hosts of painters became fashionable mimics. Seeking a bombproof shelter, they descended the staircase. Since iron courses irresistibly through all men's and nations' blood, iron now summons the painter. Can he portray iron? Can Art demolish the ivory tower and strike at the tyranny and torment which men have caused iron to bring down upon mankind?"

3. THE LATE YEARS

PAUL J. SACHS

There came an unforgettable moment in March 1947 when Paul J. Sachs unexpectedly knocked at the door of my Sixty-seventh Street studio. Greetings exchanged, he examined my pictures. Silently I awaited the master's verdict. His scrutiny finally settled on one canvas about the size and shape of a *cassone* I own attributed to Gozzoli. (How I got that superb picture for a song is another story.)

"Forgive me if I offend you," Sachs said at last, "but this is two pictures," and he ran a finger perpendicularly across the canvas. At once I saw how right he was and cut the canvas in two. Thereupon he bought the piece on the left; refusing to accept it for himself, he gave it to the Walker Art Center of Minneapolis. I named it *The Survivors*. The other part is in the

Jewish Museum, a fine institution created by Frieda, widow of Felix Warburg.

"Why not quit the law entirely if you can afford to do so," Sachs inquired, "and devote the rest of your life to painting?" I could hardly believe my ears. That this man thought enough of my paintings to offer so startling a suggestion was a bigger bombshell than had been Warburg's 1921 invitation to go to Europe. Warburg had asked only for a year's absence from the law. Sachs was proposing a final parting of the ways.

I did not deceive myself. At the Bar I believed I not only had a secure place, but could continue to be an actor in the main current of life if I chose to buckle down to the law. I foresaw that there might be days when, sitting solitary in my studio while others were in the thick of battle, I might suffer what Robert Louis Stevenson once called "the impure passion of remorse." Though the Fogg Museum had for years encouraged my painting efforts and owned many of my paintings, pastels, and lithographs, it was almost my only collector. Elsewhere I had had scant recognition. I knew, as Paul J. Sachs has put it in an introduction to a recent book by James Thrall Soby, that "many American collectors tend without a trace of passionate conviction, to toe a line dictated by fashion," and that my landscapes were therefore out of the running. In the foreword to my 1950 one-man show at the Fogg Museum, John Coolidge wrote that, "The majority of Rosenberg's works are landscapes. This is a comparatively unpopular subject among American painters today." The truth of this observation I had long recognized.

Weighing all these factors I nevertheless ended my association with the law firm which I had headed for over thirty active years. I have never since entered a courtroom or accepted a retainer and have resisted all temptations to put on the harness of the law. I have never regretted that decision.

THE NEGEV TOMORROW: Oil, 1951 : Collection Senator and Mrs. Herbert H. Lehman, New York

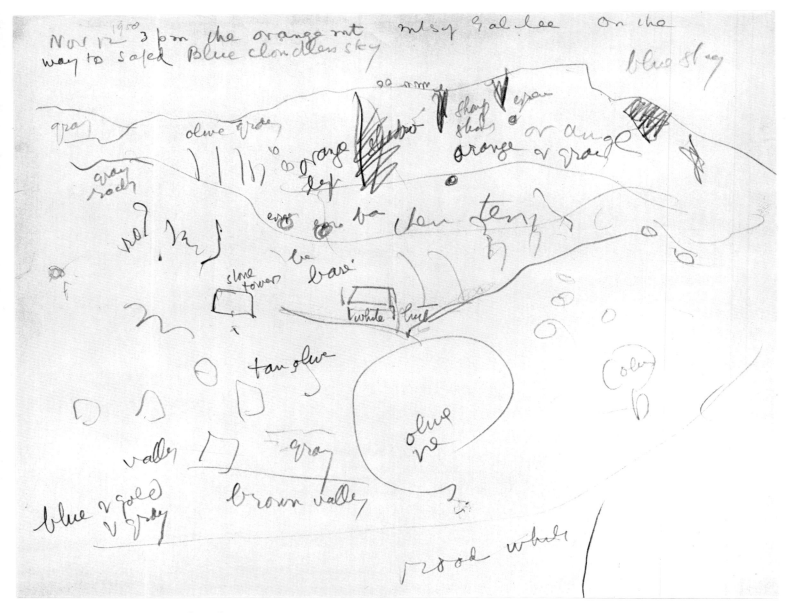

SKETCH WITH NOTES : Pencil, 1950 : The artist

Sometime thereafter Sachs, as I later learned from others, attended a meeting of art directors and curators in Washington. What he said or did there I never found out. But distinguished visitors began coming to my studio. David E. Finley, the creative, able builder and then the director of our nation's great National Gallery of Art (now, by appointment of President Eisenhower, chairman of a national committee designed to acquaint the world with our country's art); John Walker, then the National Gallery's chief curator, now its director; and Duncan Phillips, founder of his own fine museum, were the first of such guests. Coming together, they overwhelmed me. They selected and I was overjoyed to give them three of my large landscapes for the Smithsonian Institution, parent body of the National Gallery (the latter being forbidden to own works of art until twenty years after the artist's death), two for the Phillips Museum. Here was recognition such as I had never dreamed of.

Mr. Walker also chose Adirondack landscapes for embassies in London, Paris, and Rio. Others came to see me. Among them were W. G. Constable, William M. Milliken, Charles G. Cunningham, John Coolidge, Adelyn Breeskin. They either purchased or accepted gifts of my pictures. Recently Mr. Finley chose eight more of my Adirondack landscapes for U.S. embassies and Mr. Walker acquired three additional landscapes for the Smithsonian, reserving to the National Gallery the right to own them when they are "eligible for inclusion in the permanent collection by nature of the fact that you have been dead for twenty years." Recalling my eightieth birthday, when the late John W. Davis congratulated me on having become an "octogeranium," and hoped I might bloom for some more years, I am in no hurry to have those pictures become "eligible."

Visits came also from dealers, all of which led to one-man shows, to some sales (the highest price I ever asked for or got was $600), and to acquisitions by a few collectors and a good many museums.

THE METROPOLITAN MUSEUM OF ART

The 1922 New Gallery adventure and the W.P.A. formed in 1933 enabled me, as a member of the New York Committee, headed by the late Juliana Force, to view the works of some 700 of our artists to whom, while Federal funds lasted, we paid thirty-eight dollars a week to keep them from selling apples on street corners. I was convinced that many of those artists were doing fine things and was determined to help them, if ever I could, to gain recognition. Much as I have always admired the art of France, I became deeply concerned nine years ago, because our great Metropolitan Museum of Art was not only neglecting, but banishing, all living art, particularly that of our country.

This background explains my indignation when in 1949 I read an *Atlantic Monthly* article by Francis Henry Taylor, powerful director at the time of the Metropolitan Museum, in which he asserted that the art of the U.S.A. "announces the sterility and intellectual vacuum of twentieth-century America," and that "the innocent layman visiting national exhibitions may be forgiven for suspecting that the chief purpose of American art is to illustrate the Kinsey report."

Shocked because neither the trustees of the great Metropolitan Museum nor our artists or art associations raised their voices in protest, I made a study of contracts which the Metropolitan Museum had entered into with the Museum of Modern

Art and the Whitney Museum, whereby the Metropolitan had fled from contemporary American artists as if they were lepers. When I also found that the Museum had long neglected to use the Hearn funds, given almost half a century ago for purchase of works of living American artists, I prepared and daily sent nine open letters (January 6 to 14, 1949) to Roland L. Redmond, the Museum's president, which sharply criticized the Museum and reached the press. My carefully documented letters, prepared after much study, made a considerable hullabaloo. They were, so to speak, a lawyer's brief in behalf of living artists, chiefly those of the U.S.A.

This is water long over the dam. Since the publication of my letters the Museum has, under the able direction of Robert Beverley Hale, who was then made head of the Department of American Art, acquired over five hundred modern American works, traditional and advanced, ranging all the way from Grandma Moses to Jackson Pollock. This has lately led to another and very different open letter from me to Mr. Redmond (published in the May 1957 issue of *ARTS*), urging the Museum to erect a noble American building for permanent display of our country's art from its pre-Revolutionary beginnings, so that the world can thereby learn that the U.S.A. is not merely a financial octopus.

The Museum has printed this letter for public distribution, along with *A Reply from the President together with a statement by the Director relating to the Museum's plans for the exhibition of American painting and sculpture.* "I am heartily in favor of your plan to provide adequate quarters at the Metropolitan Museum for the exhibition of American paintings and sculpture," Mr. Redmond wrote, in part. "The Board of Trustees would welcome such a development and Mr. Rorimer has been authorized to explore the possibility of constructing an important addition to the Museum adjacent to the wing which houses our collections of American decorative arts." And able Director Rorimer hopes that the encouragement of friends of the Museum will "take a tangible form that will permit the Trustees to broaden our program." Will a Lorenzo di Medici or a Maecenas of our era immortalize himself, I had asked in that open letter, by giving the few million dollars needed for such a building? I hope for an answer to my question.

America, I wrote in 1922, "needs its artists as much as its artists need America." That statement not only holds true, but today has even more significance than it had thirty-five years ago. The fact that the Museum has lately appointed this gadfly to a fellowship "in perpetuity" evidences not only the gracious and open-minded spirit of its officers and trustees but, what is far more important, its devotion to the cause of our country's art. The broad vision of its director, James J. Rorimer, who created the magnificent Cloisters but opens the doors to contemporary abstract art, is a heartening proof of the Museum's present far-seeing policies and purposes.

MUSEUM OF MODERN ART

This brings me to the Museum of Modern Art, of which in 1929 I was happy to be one of the founding members. Its needed championship of experimentation, no matter who the artist or what his beliefs, politics, nationality, or art; its wide range of activities; its publications; above all, its powerful trustees and curators, men and women of great prestige, have made it an immensely influential taste-maker the world over. The Museum's director, René D'Harnoncourt, made no overstatement when in 1954 he wrote that it has "played an important role in the cultural life of the city, the nation and the world."

The Museum of Modern Art's 1939 tenth-anniversary exhibition, wisely "planned especially for visitors to the World's Fair," was modestly entitled "Art in Our Time." It showed paintings and sculptures "divided about equally between American and European work of the past seventy years." But a decade later came a profound change of policy and outlook evidenced by its 1950 booklet entitled *Collection des Maîtres*, published in France and evidently designed for world-wide distribution. This little book contains reproductions of fifty-eight works of which only nine are by Americans.

Its relegation of the art of our country to a very secondary place became even more pronounced in 1954 in its 25th Anniversary Loan Exhibition proudly titled "Masters of Modern Art." That widely attended show opened with a letter from President Eisenhower and consisted largely of "paintings from private collections," loaned by the Museum's trustees themselves. Thus it displayed the taste of these eminent personages.

In the foreword to the impressive volume which the Museum published, John Hay Whitney, the Museum's chairman, stated: "Particularly during a time when conformity enforced through authoritarian pressure is a constant threat to the development of a free society, it is most heartening to turn to the arts and to find in them the vitality and diversity that reflects freedom of thought and faith. . . . This freedom we believe fundamental to democratic society."

How did those glowing words square with the 1954 exhibition? The catalogue lists one hundred and fifty-nine pieces, of which only thirteen were of our native art: while one hundred and forty-six were by foreign artists—fourteen of Matisse, twenty of Picasso.

This humble and minor place for our country's art in

that all important 25th Anniversary Exhibition was in contrast with the principles and purposes well stated by Mr. Whitney, and was, I hold, a mistaken policy, especially in these times when totalitarian powers seek to control men's minds. Our dramatists, architects, and composers need not and do not play second fiddle. Neither need our artists do so.

A century ago Nathaniel Hawthorne longed for an America "free from the shadow of Europe." As long ago as the eighteen forties, Edgar Allan Poe wrote, "We have at length arrived at that epoch when our literature may and must stand on its own merits or fall through its own defects. We have snapped asunder the leading-strings of our British grandmama." Are those same strings today making the art of our country subservient to the art of France? In his 1957 *A History of France* (Farrar, Straus and Cudahy) André Maurois wrote that "the great American museums, in particular so far as contemporary movements are concerned, have become museums of French Art." The introduction to the magnificent Museum of Modern Art volume in celebration of its twenty-fifth anniversary contains a sentence worth quoting here. "Museum people are notoriously blind," wrote Alfred H. Barr, Jr. director of the Museum collection. To whom did he refer? Let us hope that this powerful institution will return to its wise policies of 1939.

HOSPITALS

An auction sale in 1949 at Wildenstein Galleries for benefit of the New York United Hospital Fund marked a new adventure for me. For that sale I gave one of my landscapes at the request of Ilka Chase. One of the pictures offered for sale brought no bidder. It was a *cassone*. Miss Chase then put it in the hands of an important dealer. When no bid came she asked me to buy it. I did so, telling her that as I thought it of value I would gladly also give a few dozen more of my pictures to the United Hospital Fund. This I did; and few things have given me more satisfaction than a letter I received from a hospital patient saying that my picture cheered him. This has led to similar gifts to Boston, New York, Cleveland, and Hartford hospitals. My paintings are in a good many museums. From now on I'd rather give them to hospitals and am doing so. Psychiatrists tell me that pictures help their patients. The thought of giving such help means more to me than selling a picture.

As for the *cassone*, I believe it to be a great masterpiece. Though it has long been attributed to Gozzoli, my own studies (though I claim no expertness) incline me to think it is a Sassetta.

ARTS MAGAZINE

Thirty-five years ago I helped Peyton Boswell to found *Art Digest* (now *ARTS*) because he was a believer in art wherever created and whatever its aims. When both he and his son died, the magazine landed on the rocks. At my instance an able young man, Jonathan Marshall, grandson of my beloved friend Louis Marshall, came to the rescue. Marshall became its publisher and I became chairman of its board but take no part in its management. Very occasionally I have written for it, as for example when I discussed Cézanne's credo or when Harry N. Abrams brought his admirable fifty-cent art pocket books to millions of people.

Two years ago, when the U.S.I.A. (United States Information Agency) outrageously forbade exhibitions of American paintings selected by American Federation of Arts; would not allow a Toscanini-founded orchestra to go overseas on the alleged ground that some of the artists or musicians were or might be fellow travelers or Communists; and when the American Federation of Arts and musicians' organizations seemed to surrender to this inexcusable censorship, we became busy. The result was our open letter to President Eisenhower, published in *ARTS*.

Recalling therein the President's eloquent message, in 1954, for the twenty-fifth anniversary of the Museum of Modern Art, in which he announced that "freedom of the arts is a basic freedom, one of the pillars of liberty in our land," we urged that:

> *"The free world is presently engaged in a crucial battle for the hearts and minds of men. Among America's greatest assets in this struggle are our cultural heritage and achievements. When these are silenced, we not only stifle creative art, we forfeit the respect of people in other lands. . . .*
>
> *"We hope therefore that you will intervene so that these acts of censorship will not obliterate the freedoms guaranteed by the Bill of Rights."*

Though our letter received no acknowledgment, the President has since then appointed a new man—George V. Allen—to head U.S.I.A. Let us hope that henceforth the freedoms guaranteed us will be honored with something more than high-sounding words. It is an endless battle.

Many fine words have been written about the urgent need of acquainting the world with our art. Congress has called for dissemination of our culture. President Eisenhower has created his "People to People Program." Committees of leading citizens have been set up. But the lack of what I consider effective action is a challenge to those of us who believe that the world ought to be informed about the notable art of our country.

PATHS AND BY-PATHS

For good or bad, many more lures than the dazzling bits of fur and feather and tinsel in my trout-fly boxes have continually dragged me from my easel. There has been the non-profit Artists Gallery, admirably directed by Hugh Stix, giving unknown artists their first opportunity to exhibit their works. There was the 1949 petition to Secretary of State Acheson, presented by a committee which I formed. We sought to free Cardinal Mindszenty from prison. Mr. Acheson made a vigorous but futile effort to rouse the timid United Nations to action. There was the unsuccessful effort led at my request by a great man, the late Robert P. Patterson, to persuade the U.S. Senate to ratify the Genocide Convention, as most of the member states of the United Nations have already done. The deplorable opposition of the American Bar Association was chiefly responsible for failure.

There was the settlement of Jews in the Dominican Republic marked by generous and unfailing support of Generalissimo Trujillo, who gave our Settlement Association his magnificent 26,000-acre property at Sosua. There the settlers who escaped from Hitler are now self-supporting citizens of the land which opened its doors to them. There were continual battles against anti-Semites; there was my 1948 visit to England with Everett R. Clinchy (with whom I had long worked for the National Conference of Christians and Jews) and Henry Noble MacCracken to launch a movement called World

Brotherhood, which seeks to bring to the world's grass roots a sense of reality and meaning in the concept of man's brotherhood. There was my thrilling 1950 visit to Israel in company with Ambassador McDonald, which produced a spate of pictures. There was the sorrowful luncheon at Rehovoth as guest of my old friend, the sick and dying Chaim Weizmann, who said to me as I bade him a last farewell, "So now you see that all the 'lies' we Zionists told you about Jewish life in Palestine were only half the truth." There followed my day at the shore of the Sea of Galilee (upon whose waters Jesus trod) with David Ben-Gurion—of whom I painted a portrait now in Jerusalem—happy

PORTRAIT OF DAVID BEN-GURION: Oil, 1950: The artist

because that very morning he had at long last acquired fifty volumes of works of Greek philosophers in the original Greek.

The gaunt Galilean mountains; the *Kibbutzim* (Israel farm settlements); the desert Negev, the pipe lines bringing it water; the long ride from Dan to Beersheba; Safed, Nazareth, and Haifa; the crowded city of Tel Aviv; the ancient olive trees; the Balfour forests promising that fifty years of peace will transform the barren peaks of both Israel and Arab lands into verdant life-giving Adirondacks; the steep road to Jerusalem—these were but a few of the sights which produced landscapes, most of which I have given to Jewish institutions.

There was the 1955 World Brotherhood assemblage of 500 men and women at Brussels, made possible by a letter written by my friend John J. McCloy (I had first met him when he was a junior partner in the great Cravath law firm) to several hundred people with whom I had worked, asking for World Brotherhood gifts in celebration of my eightieth birthday. There was my visit to that meeting, carrying a message from John Foster Dulles, and there followed my motor ride through the Ardennes on the way to a Belgian trout stream.

The haunting memory of endless white crosses of unknown soldiers who lay beneath the blood-soaked terrain of the Ardennes produced another series of paintings exhibited in 1955 at the AAA Galleries in New York, titled "Paintings of Two Worlds"—the happy Adirondacks on the one hand, on the other the threat of nuclear war.

In 1941 International Business Machines Corporation published a book entitled *Contemporary Art of the Western Hemisphere*. It listed 103 pictures owned by IBM, all of them painted by artists of twenty-two Western Hemisphere nations. Mr. Thomas J. Watson's memorable foreword, which concluded with an affirmation of "faith that through the language of the artist, people will be better able to recognize those traits common to all men which bind humanity together in universal kinship," is in considerable measure the *raison d'être* of this chapter. Thus when art lovers in Israel begged me in 1950 to arrange an exhibition of current Israeli art for the United States, I remembered Mr. Watson and was glad to help bring about a fine exhibition of Israeli paintings at the Metropolitan Museum.

Again in 1952 an exhibition in New York of current Indonesian paintings gave me another opportunity to put Mr. Watson's idea into action. Indonesian Ambassador Ali Sastroamidjojo was in New York. I gave a reception in his honor at my home and had the Indonesian paintings on my walls. Among my guests were leaders in the art world. The expressions of gratitude of my Indonesian guests because we Americans were glad to see and respect their contemporary art made an indelible impression on my mind.

Our government, having embarked on a policy of cultural exchanges with nations, including the Soviet Union, why not have traveling exhibitions of outstanding American paintings and sculpture; why not have American paintings on the walls of our embassies and consulates? (To cite one instance, neither our embassy at The Hague, nor the Carnegie Peace Palace, have a single painting on their walls.) Will our overcrowded museums lend our government some of their

American paintings, in order to help show the world our native art?

Particularly why not follow the example of leading American corporations, which have distributed, gratis, to their employees, millions of art booklets, beautifully illustrated in color? If American industry finds it wise to do this, why do we not do it as a nation? At modest cost such booklets, with one or two dozen color reproductions of famous American paintings, can be at the reception desk of every American embassy and elsewhere throughout the entire world, as spokesmen for that "universal kinship" which mankind craves.

Neither our military triumphs in two World Wars, nor those who gave their lives, nor our political or diplomatic efforts—not even our astronomic outpourings of treasure—have brought us the kind of world we want to live in. Where missiles and atom bombs fail, art may perhaps achieve something. Toward that end is my absorbing, unfinished business.

FINALE

It is a May day. At long last my writing efforts have ended. This morning I wandered down to my two-acre pond at Scarsdale, the home of mallard and wood ducks, large-mouth bass, blue gills, blue jays, chickadees, and cardinal birds. On the tiny isle in the middle of the pond a Canadian wild goose has built her nest. Her spouse guards her. The mallard gentlemen are pursuing the ladies. The bass are spawning. The swamp maples wear crimson jewels. Our fruit trees, bursting into a million blossoms, remind me that we humans cannot put forth new leaves and blossoms when comes springtime.

As I now review what I have written and note the many inevitable repetitions of the personal pronoun, I can only indulge the hope that the accounts of my diverse adventures through my long years, even when not facing a rectangle of canvas, have been a relevant part of this painter's story.

Should I, as in 1921, have refused to write this story? Perhaps so; yet there are things which I felt ought to be said. As for my pictures, I am aware that no words of mine can help them to live. Whatever their fate, I am content. My landscapes have been and are magic carpets on which I have flown from a world embittered by fear, hate, and greed, to regions of peace, joy, and beauty. For which I humbly give thanks.

The Pictures

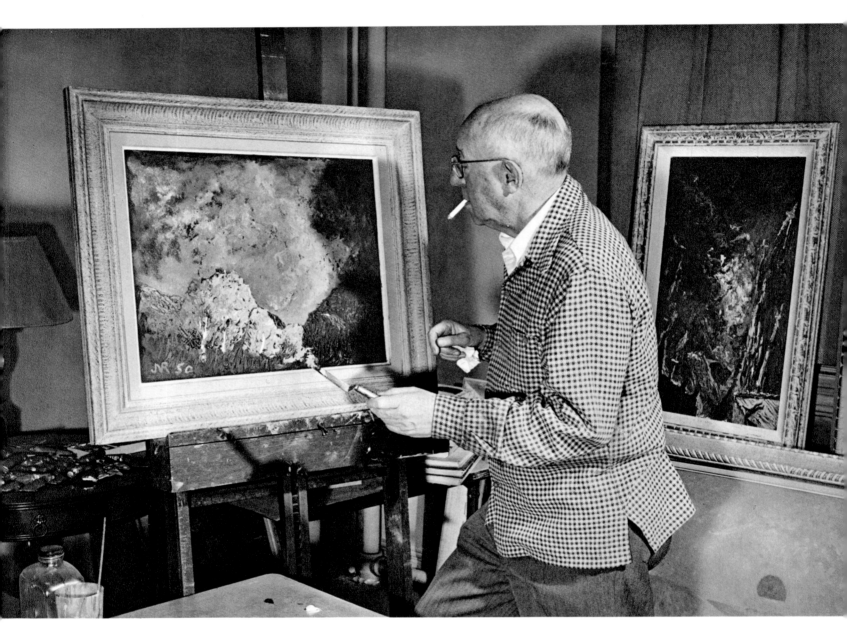

Photograph by Sidney Weintraub, New York

FOURTEENTH STREET FROM GEO. MILLER'S PLACE: Lithograph,
1919: Fogg Art Museum, Harvard University, Cambridge, Massachusetts

ADIRONDACK LAKE: Lithograph, 1919: Metropolitan Museum of Art, New York

ADIRONDACKS : Lithograph, 1919 : Smithsonian Institution, Washington, D.C.

FROM MOUNT MONADNOCK: Pastel, 1921 : The artist

DELAWARE WATER GAP: Pastel, 1921 : The artist

LANDSCAPE: Oil, about 1921: Fogg Art Museum, Harvard University, Cambridge, Massachusetts

"THE STRENGTH OF THE HILLS IS HIS": Oil, about 1924 : Whereabouts unknown

WALKING RAIN: Lithograph, 1929: Metropolitan Museum of Art, New York

ADIRONDACK TREES : Oil, 1928 : Whereabouts unknown

CHANGING WEATHER : Oil, 1936 : Whereabouts unknown

SALMON RIVER: Oil, 1936: United States Department of State

MIST IN THE ORCHARDS: Oil, about 1937: Collection Mrs. James N. Rosenberg, Scarsdale, New York

DELAWARE WATER GAP: Pastel, 1921: Collection Mr. and Mrs. Milton S. Fox, Scarsdale, New York

BOUQUET RIVER : Oil, mid-1930s : Whereabouts unknown

SWIFT SHOWER : Pastel, 1935 : Whereabouts unknown

HISTORY OF MY PEOPLE: Pastel, 1927: The artist

DARK YOUNG FOREST : Pastel, about 1930 : Whereabouts unknown

ADIRONDACK MOONRISE: Oil, 1944: The artist

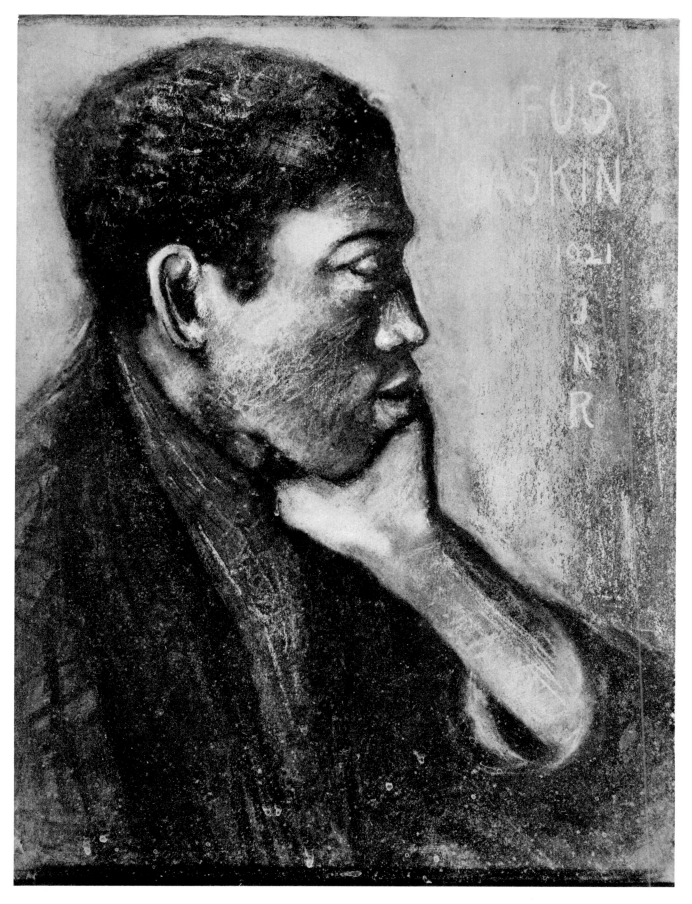

PORTRAIT OF RUFUS GASKIN : Pastel, 1921 : Fogg Art Museum, Harvard University, Cambridge, Massachusetts

BLACK EYES: Oil, about 1922: The artist

PORTRAIT OF FRATER SPIRIDON: Pastel,
1921 : Fogg Art Museum, Harvard University,
Cambridge, Massachusetts

WAYMAN ADAMS AT THE FAIR: Oil,
about 1924 : Collection Elizabethtown Community Center, Elizabethtown, New York

SHOLOM ASCH: Pastel, 1922: The artist

TWO YOUNG AMERICANS: Pastel, about 1921 : Collection
Essex County Historical Society, Elizabethtown, New York

MANY PORTRAITS OF LOUIS UNTERMEYER: Oil,
1929: The artist

PORTRAIT OF GEORGE HAYES: Oil, about 1928 : Collection Millard Hayes,
Elizabethtown, New York

BAR HARBOR: Watercolor, early 1920s: Whereabouts unknown

CORSICAN LANDSCAPE: Watercolor, 1934: Whereabouts unknown

MOUNTAIN LANDSCAPE, CORSICA:
Watercolor, 1934: Collection Mr. and Mrs. Robert Rosenberg, White Plains, New York

CORSICAN MOUNTAIN VILLAGE: Watercolor, 1934 : Collection Dr. Elizabeth Zetzel, Cambridge, Massachusetts

PALM BEACH: Watercolor, about 1940: Whereabouts unknown

ADIRONDACK MORNING: Watercolor, 1949: Whereabouts unknown

SNOW IN THE CITY: Oil, 1946: The Cleveland Museum of Art, Cleveland, Ohio

PITTSBURGH (Ironism series) : Pastel, 1943 : Whereabouts unknown

PITTSBURGH VICTORY GARDEN (Ironism series) : Pastel, 1943 :
Whereabouts unknown

INGOT FARM (Ironism series) : Pastel, 1943 : Whereabouts unknown

THE MILLS OF THE MEN (Ironism series) : Pastel, 1943 :
Whereabouts unknown

DOVE OF PEACE (Ironism series) : Pastel, 1943 : Whereabouts unknown

MAGNIFICENCE OF WAR (Ironism series) : Pastel, 1943 :
Georgia Museum of Art, Athens, Georgia

THE MASTER RACE PAYS A VISIT (Ironism series) : Pastel, 1943 : Whereabouts unknown

"CONSUMED BY THINE ANGER" (Ironism series) : Pastel, 1943 :
Fogg Art Museum, Harvard University, Cambridge, Massachusetts

SUNFLOWERS : Oil, 1930s : Whereabouts unknown

FLOWER GARDEN : Pastel, about 1940 : The artist

A BOUQUET IN THE WINDOW : Pastel, about 1940 : Whereabouts unknown

SUNFLOWERS: Oil, 1944–47: United States Embassy, Rio de Janeiro, Brazil

LATE SUNSHINE: Oil, 1957: Collection Mr. and Mrs. Marshall Lee, Flemington, New Jersey

HIROSHIMA (Atomism series) : Oil, 1945 : Fogg Art Museum,
Harvard University, Cambridge, Massachusetts

WALL STREET (Atomism series) : Oil, 1945–47 :
Whereabouts unknown

PEACE ON EARTH: Montage, oil and paper, 1948: The artist

IS THIS THE MAN THAT MADE THE EARTH TO TREMBLE? (Ironism series):
Pastel, 1944: Whereabouts unknown

THE MIST AND THE RAIN: Oil, about 1950: Whereabouts unknown

DRAWING: Pencil, 1947: The artist

STORM CLOUDS: Oil, 1947 : National Collection of Art, Smithsonian Institution, Washington, D.C.

LAKE PLACID: Oil, 1943: Mrs. James N. Rosenberg, Scarsdale. New York

THE BIG RAIN : Oil, 1944 : Collection Dr. Maurice B. Hexter, New York

ADIRONDACKS IN OCTOBER: Oil, about 1940 : Philbrook Art Center, Tulsa, Oklahoma

THREE OR FOUR TREES: Oil, 1946: Whereabouts unknown

ADIRONDACK WINTER: Oil, 1948–49: Collection Mr. and Mrs. Robert Rosenberg, White Plains, New York

THE ATLANTIC AT EASTHAMPTON: Oil, 1949: Mrs. James N. Rosenberg, Scarsdale, New York

YOUNG FOREST: Oil, 1944: Fogg Art Museum, Harvard University, Cambridge, Massachusetts

SHAGGY TREES: Oil, 1950: Estate of Felix Wildenstein

THE BIG WAVE: Pencil, 1949: Metropolitan Museum of Art, New York

HURRICANE: Oil, about 1938: Whereabouts unknown

SLANTING RAIN: Oil, 1946: Nelson Gallery-Atkins Museum,
Kansas City, Missouri

SOMBER DUSK: Oil, 1940: Whereabouts unknown

BLUE STREAM: Oil, 1952 : Collection Mr. and Mrs. Harry N. Abrams, New York

THE CLOUDS ROLL BY: Oil, 1945 : Bowdoin College Museum of Fine Arts, Brunswick, Maine

BLUE STREAM: Oil, 1952 : Collection Mr. and Mrs. Harry N. Abrams, New York

THE CLOUDS ROLL BY : Oil, 1945 : Bowdoin College Museum of Fine Arts, Brunswick, Maine

ADIRONDACKS: Oil, 1946: National Collection of Art, Smithsonian Institution, Washington, D.C.

AUTUMN HEAT—EVENING: Oil, 1945: Springfield Museum of Fine Arts, Springfield, Massachusetts

ABANDONED FARM: Oil, 1945: Collection Mr. and Mrs. Robert Beverly Hale, New York

COBBLE HILL: Oil, 1947: Collection Dr. and Mrs. Harry C. Solomon, Boston, Massachusetts

GREEN APRIL : Oil, about 1943 : Museum of Fine Arts, Boston, Massachusetts

MOUNTAIN ROAD: Oil, 1945: Whereabouts unknown

TREE PATTERNS: Oil, 1949: Collection Mr. and Mrs. John Walker, Washington, D.C.

THE OLD HORSE: Oil, 1948 : Collection Mrs. Katherine Seiden, Tuckahoe, New York

BIG STORM : Oil, 1951 : Whereabouts unknown

SEA OF GALILEE: Oil, 1951: American Jewish Congress

WHITE CLIFFS OF LEBANON: Oil, 1950 : Collection Dr. Elizabeth Zetzel, Cambridge, Massachusetts

MT. ATZMOND FROM SAFED : Oil, 1950 : The artist

THE YOUNG SABRAS: Oil, 1953: The artist

KOREAN SPRING MORNING (Atomism series) : Oil, 1951 :
Whereabouts unknown

NUCLEAR NIGHTMARE (Atomism series): Oil, 1952 : The artist

FLIGHT TO NOWHERE (Atomism series) : Oil, 1953 : Whereabouts unknown

WINDY MORNING: Oil, about 1952 : United States Department of State

AUSABLE LAKE: Crayon, 1953: Whereabouts unknown

MISTY SPRING MORNING: Pastel on velvet paper, 1954: Whereabouts unknown

THE ANCIENT OLIVE TREE, ISRAEL : Crayon, 1953 :
Collection Mr. and Mrs. Maxwell Geismar, Harrison, New York

BEECH TREES : Crayon, 1953 : Whereabouts unknown

SHANTY BROOK SPRINGTIME : Oil, 1948–50 : Georgia Museum of Art, Athens, Georgia

THE GODS AND THE ATOM (Ardennes series) : Oil, 1955 : The artist

NUCLEAR TRIUMPH (Atomism series) : Oil, 1954 : The artist

PLUMED KNIGHT AND THE MUSHROOM CLOUD (Ardennes series):
Oil, 1955: Whereabouts unknown

SALMON RIVER: Pastel, 1944: Estate of John W. Davis

FALLS BROOK IN FLOOD: Oil, 1947: Fogg Art Museum,
Harvard University, Cambridge, Massachusetts

JACKSON BROOK: Oil, about 1940: Whereabouts unknown

DOWNPOUR: Oil, about 1950: United States Department of State

SUNNY SEPTEMBER: Oil, 1954 : Collection Mr. and Mrs. Milton S. Fox, Scarsdale, New York

SUMMER CAFÉ : Oil, 1949 : The artist

GLORIOUS SNOWSTORM : Oil, 1954 : The artist

ADIRONDACK PINES : Oil, 1953 : Collection Mr. and Mrs. Alfred Hecht, Harrison, New York

MOHAWK TRAIL : Oil, 1956 : Whereabouts unknown

Appendix

ROMAN HOLIDAY *

Conversation Piece, 1926

I

Signore Alcide Battacioli,
My cyclopedic guide,
Affirms that Rome's the home
Of thirty thousand churches.
Amazing his researches;
To the metre
He knows the height
Of every monument to Paul or Peter;
Of every soaring spire.
Whereas I only know
They would have to go
Infinitely higher
Lifted by God's leaven
To reach the door of heaven.

* *Reprinted by permission, from The Menorah Journal, Volume xxxv, Number 2, April 1947.*

II

Brolio Barone Ricasoli
Vino Rosso Da Pasto:
That is a red, red, ruddy, heady wine.
It marches,
Swerves and lurches
Through my blood
From head to feet of mine.
Twenty-five lire only;
La Bottiglia cheers the lonely.
The Ulpia, bronze Basilica
In Hadrian's day,
Is now a gay café,
Sought out by tourists who enjoy
Good food and drinking;
They quaff their Brolio,
Also Oporto di Spagna; Capri Scala;
Vini di Sardegna; Bianco Marsala.
Such exquisite essences suspend
And put at least a temporary end
To thinking.

III

To thinking? Do they?
For I somehow find
That wretched swastika still glued
To my mind.
That cursed swastika,
Which some Nazi varlet,
An insane dog,
Daubed with scarlet paint
On the tall wall
Of Frankfort's ancient synagogue,
Where once my great-grandfather
Worshiped.

IV

In Berlin I told them about it,
My hosts; important men,

Eight or a dozen or ten.
Chairmen and Presidents
Of every Jewish Committee
In their rich and important city.
Men of kind hearts and pity.
They flouted and scouted my fear;
They doubted
Whether anything
Ought to be done about it.
They would not hear
Me when I pled.
It was a mere incident, they said,
A trifling incident, wholly
Beneath notice.
Waiter, the Ricasoli.

V

I. N. R. I.
S. P. Q. R.
Rafael and his Fornarina,
Pier Luigi da Palestrina.
Paolo and Francesca;
Dante, San Tommaso d'Aquina,
A thousand names
Make echoes in my ear.
Leonardo and Botticelli
And also Machiavelli;
But especially
Percy Bysshe Shelley.
This morning at his Roman bier
A shame-faced tear
For just an instant
Restored my youth;
When I believed I had found
In Prometheus Unbound
The holy ground where flourish
Justice, freedom, beauty, and truth.

V I

Yes, there is education in these tours.
Iesus Nazarenus Rex Iudeorum—

Is he my King or yours,
Noble Alcide?
I plead; give me an answer,
Philosopher and guide.
Thirty thousand answers?
Thirty what or who?
Gentile or Jew?
Pass me the rosy bottle,
Its wisdom outlasts Aristotle.
Now I remember, good Alcide,
It was the Coliseum.
Then let us chant a great Te Deum
For thirty thousand Jews:
For thirty thousand slaves
Who, you declare,
Builded that edifice there;
Beneath its stones their graves.

VII

There in that sweat and clamor,
Broken by whip and hammer,
Look! Do you see a great-
Great-grandfather of mine?
Old, old; yes older
Than Amos or Adam;
Crushed by weight
Of boulder on shoulder.
He is one of a shackled crew,
Every man jack of them a Jew.
They drag great granite columns
Along a stony path (blood-spattered,
As if that mattered)
To Caracalla's bath.
Thirty thousand? Every one a Jew?
Alcide, that scarcely can be true.

VIII

But see; by all that's holy! Ho!
There sits the poet, Horace.
I recognize his features,

SURVIVORS: Oil, 1945–46 : Walker Art Center, Minneapolis, Minnesota

He sips my Brolio,
He does not see those tattered,
Shattered creatures.
He versifies into the folio
Which rests upon his knee.
Can you not see
Him scribbling now?
Beneath the ardent Roman sky
Roman youths and maidens,
Rose-garlanded,
Bathe slim,
Anointed limbs.
They chant pure hymns
To love and poesy.
Pure? I am not quite sure,
That wine of thine,
Those slow dances
And significant glances
From man to maid and maid to man
Breed strange, erotic fancies.

IX

Garlands? I see only thorns;
The garland pierces, adorns
The Prince of peace,
King of the Jews,
Rex Iudeorum, there on the cross.
What cross? With bloody feet,
Who bears it through the centuries
Up and down the Street?
That street at Frankfort;
Stony avenues of all the world;
Who bear it;
Who forever wear it
Through storm and sleet
And ice and tropic heat?

X

Ebb and flow.
They come. They go.

Fast or slow.
Now, through the red Ulpian umber,
I, who desire only slumber,
Behold the long, long, bent procession.
Through acrid fogs
They thread their way
Winter and summer,
Night and day,
Stopping only
To build their synagogues.
Jews, Jews, a million.
Maybe a billion.
Young and old; broken cripples.
Babies who suck on empty nipples;
And each one bears a crucifix,
Whether aged sixty
Or aged six.
For them no sweet digression;
No intercession.
There is little of fraternity
Or sorority
For a minority.

XI

They trod the roads of Spain;
Through German muck and rain,
Past fields of Russian grain.
They faced the Inquisition.
Say, what can be their mission?
In London I asked my British friends
Where this agelong Hegira ends.
Are we to be banned
From our promised land?
What of the British lion
When it comes to Zion?

XII

I see the living and the dead,
The roads are carmine
Where they tread.

I wait those waiting to be born;
My children's children's
Children's sons;
Will they be tortured by the Huns?
They linger in earth's womb
Waiting their turn
To be tormented and torn
From cradle to tomb.

XIII

What is it, good Alcide,
What do you whisper?
Why do you jog my arm?
"Softly, Signore;
These walls have ears;
I would not have you come to harm.
Softly, Signore, you need to heed—
A whisper to the wise—
I beg you; guard your speech.
Everywhere there are spies;
The Fascists have a long, long reach.
Moreover, loudly I declare
Fascism is holy everywhere.
Come, in solitude and quiet
Let us walk,
Out in the open we can talk,
Here there will be a riot."

XIV

Crossing the Atlantic, Alcide,
I met an anthropologist;
An educated fellow, if pedantic;
He nearly drove me frantic
Crossing the Atlantic.
"There is," said he, said he,
"No creature such as Jew," said he,
"Anthropomorphically, I mean,"
Said he, said he.
"You are no separate people.
Then why not pray

Beneath our steeple?
Neither your skull nor head,
Nor eyes are recognizable;
Though I admit," he giggled—
His wit was elephantic—
As he wiggled on his deck chair,
"Your nasal organs
Sometimes are almost as sizable
As Morgan's."

X V

Why do we choose to march then
In that long procession?
The Prophets? Moses?
Or just our noses?
What is it keeps us in line?
Alcide, I find no answer in the wine.

X V I

Yesterday, Alcide, I saw old women
And young ones
And old, old men
And nice little boys and girls
With blond or brunette curls
Mounting the Holy Steps.
Mounting on dusty knees.
The steps of St. John, the Lateran;
Steps brought, it is said,
From Pilate's abode.
All in a pattern
They mounted
The twenty-eight steps; I counted.
On dusty knees,
In holy meditation,
In ecstatic exaltation,
With piety and decorum
They adored
Each passion and station
Of their Lord,
Iesus Nazarenus, Rex Iudeorum;

They were granted indulgences.
Nine years of freedom
From punishment and pain.
That is something to gain.
Such indulgence
Lacks not refulgence.
Then why not ascend those stairs?
Only a few little prayers.
That is all you need.
What is it holds us back, Alcide?
Despite thumbscrew and rack, Alcide.
For what commandment do we bleed?
We stiff-necked Jews
Who suffer but refuse
To cede?

XVII

Yesterday
A mad old woman,
An Irish woman, the papers say,
Came all the way
To Rome
To murder Mussolini.
The aged lady sought his life
With an appropriate butcher's knife.
At once a Fascist mob cries out.
"Behold! It is a Jew who seeks
To slay our noble master."
Faster than speed of light
Ten thousand blackshirts
Armed for fight;
March on the Jewish ghetto.
They are going to sack it
And hack it to bits.
Someone is quick
And in the lucky nick
Of time the truth is out.
With curses, the mob disperses.
There remain only jeers and hoots;
And iron boots.
Only a few dozen patriarchs' beards
Are plucked out by the roots.

XVIII

That always seems to be the story
Ancient and hoary.
Always we are strangers at the gate.
We come too soon; we come too late.
We are unwanted. Wherefore? Look!
Is it because we always
Carry an unwelcome Book?
Must we be smitten
For what we have written?
Is it libel
To speak so of the Bible?

XIX

Inferiority complex?
Delusion of persecution?
No, friend, at home we boast
A Bill of Rights; a Constitution.
Which makes us equal—yes
Absolutely equal
On the inevitable day
When our ashes
Are put away.

XX

Perennius Aere? Who uttered
Those immortal words?
Horace or Virgil? I forget;
And yet,
When this basilica tumbles,
When its portal
Crumbles;
When all of Mussolini's brood,
Like pachyderms,
Are luscious food
For undiscriminating worms,
The stranger whom forever
Men make suffer—
Thereby making him ever

Tougher and tougher—
Somehow survives.
Cat o'nine thousand lives.
It really is mysterious.
Stop me, Alcide,
Am I becoming serious?
This sunny day
Should be my funny day.
My folly day, my jolly day,
I am in Rome
For a Roman holiday.

XXI

Sum it all up, *amigo mio,*
What remains?
A purple iris on a dunghill,
Poppies springing from the mud;
War, incest, death, and blood;
And victories' short-lived laughter.
What is their hereafter?
The Gods? Whose Gods?
Isis, Osiris, Zoroaster,
Jupiter, Mohammed, Zeus.
Recount them? What's the use?
Who is the eternal master?
Strange that over and over again
Persecution and endless pain,
All in the name of God,
Invariably
Visit the weak
Who turn the other cheek;
And still more strange,
Beaten and bruised,
Damnably misused,
Ever they spring anew from the sod;
And all that remains
Of Roman splendor,
Lies in these rusty ruins
Where we wander.

XXII

Here in my pocket, Alcide,
Is a bit of broken stone;
I picked it up yesterday
As I strolled alone
Along the Appian way.
Cicero and Trajan trod upon it,
Clement and Leo
Supplicated God upon it;
The feet of Caesar,
Pompey and Romulus stood upon it.
No need to peer vainly;
The footmarks are there;
Quite plainly.

XXIII

The ultimate fact is—I assure you
I am sober as a judge,
I speak objectively without a grudge—
That neither Chinese Wall
Nor Roman tower
Postpone the striking of the hour.
Submarine, aeroplane, gun;
Do they delay the setting sun?
Alcide, where is the waiter?
Please tell him
That in the ooze
Of yesterday's dictator
Lurks the green alligator.
And if he asks
What lives and who remain?
Tell him those only
Who forever feed on pain.

XXIV

What? What? My friend?
I slept again?
Ten thousand bugles wake me,
And shake me from dark dreams.

Thousands of blaring trumpets
And pimps and strumpets.
Augustus? Caesar Augustus?
From Actaeum? I hear him.
Let me see him.
"Signore, those are the taxicabs
Of Rome.
The hour is late.
Where do you dwell?
Good. I escort you
To the Grand Hotel.
A bath, as hot as you can stand it.
Just press a bell. Command it.
Ten lire buy a willing slave.
A shave. Clean linen. Dinner jacket,
The taxis make
A not unpleasant racket—
Pranzo? Dinner, Signore?
Vermouth, buono a tutte l'ore.
Pasticcio di Maccheroni,
Fagiano arrosto;
Presto,
Cassata Siciliana
Eppoi . . . il Nirvana!
All manner of viands most delicious;
All that the exacting palate wishes.
Asti spumante . . . liquid honey.
I tell you, sir,
When all is said and done
There still can be a little fun.
Signore, there is no question
There is nothing like a good digestion
And a pocket full of money."

XXV

Sapristi!
Lacrymae Christi!
It can dispel and soon expel
The vilest case
Of lacrymae rerum
And send a harum scarum
Sort of feeling

Stealing over you.
A farewell banquet?
A Lucullan feast?
Tomorrow, Alcide, I leave
The Fascist beast.
I have a notion
He will not follow me
Across the ocean.
Grieve not. I shall return, Alcide.
And then
We shall not heed
Inquisitive eyes
Or smirking spies
Now lurking everywhere.
There will be freedom in the air
Or else I am no Jewish prophet.
What do you say, Alcide?
"Sir, take me with you.
Take me from this Tophet."
What? Tophet? Alcide?
Art thou a Jew?
"Did you not know, Signore?
Take me to any place
Where to be Jew is to find peace,
Dignity and grace."

XXVI

Signore Alcide, you ask too much;
There is no such
Except—
"Except, Signore?"
The question leapt.
I tapped the upper region of his vest,
"Except, Signore?" he pled.
"There," I said;
"There in the unconquerable breast.
Brother, let us break bread,
And toast our brothers—
The unconquerable living,
And those others:
Our unconquerable dead."